Acclaim for *Beyond the Pews*

"*Jillian Maas Backman is a gifted intuitive, a generous and amazing empath, and a treasured teacher who brings all of those characteristics and qualities into each of our homes with her new autobiography and spiritual guidebook,* **Beyond the Pews.** *Now a new face on the publishing scene, Backman empowers each of us with her hands-on best life blueprint while also showing each of us how to easily but very effectively develop our own innate intuitive abilities. A fascinating read and a tremendously powerful tool to make dreams come true!*"

> — Ellen Whitehurst, bestselling author of *Make This Your Lucky Day* and CEO of Experience Your Extraordinary Life (www.ellenwhitehurst.com)

"*In* **Beyond The Pews** *Jillian Maas Backman delicately and necessarily bridges the gap between religion and spirituality, showing that there is no difference at all when you listen to the inner voice and follow your heart. Her personal trials and discoveries inspired her to embrace her true essence. She encourages her readers to seek their own answers as she provides guidance along the path of creative self-discovery and ignites that which already exists within.*"

> — April Claxton, CEO and Founder of The Movement Within, author of *The Movement Within: 8 Steps to Ignite The Movement Within You* and *The Power of Self Love: A Mini Book*

"This book is part biography, part poetry, and all spiritual guidance. It's the story of the growth of an intuitive, and it's a workbook for readers to come to understand and contribute to the essential interdependence of human and angelic beings. Backman writes with color and grace, and invites us all on a journey of pure joy."

— Louise Marley, author of *Mozart's Blood* and *The Brahms Deception*

"Beyond the Pews is a beautifully written, illuminating book. The author's experiences and lessons she offers to readers reveal the essential love that is God—the medicine that can cure all."

— Swami Mohan Das Bairagi

"Jillian Mass Backman is an intuitive explorer; her unique exercises show you how to become aware of the presence of divine intuition in nature, in yourself, and in other people. Beyond the Pews is filled with psychic-spiritual epiphanies and insightful exercises for increasing intuition and appreciating the awesomeness of life."

— Dennis Fairchild, author of *The Kitchen Tarot* and *The Fortune-telling Handbook*

"Jillian Maas Backman is an extraordinary teacher. For years she has been guiding her clients along the path of self-discovery to peace and understanding. Now her astounding book, Beyond the Pews, is destined to transform countless more lives."

— Susan Murphy Milano, violence expert, author of *Times Up: How to Escape Abusive and Stalking Relationships Guide*

For my mother,
the most brave and courageous woman I know.

Thank you for always supporting me in your quiet,
simple ways; I noticed.

Acknowledgments

Iam sincerely grateful to Lake Street Press, Mary Osborne, and Hazel Dawkins for their blessed talents of creative writing and editing. It was their unwavering commitment which allowed me to express, through words, thoughts I have carried inside my soul for many years. I am thankful for all my mentors who have graciously shared their insights without hesitation. Their wisdom helped define the voice I have in the world today. My heart is filled with soulful love and gratitude for my dearest family members' and friends' steadfast belief in the work I was called to do and for the protection they provided. I thank those I have lost along the journey—Bruce, Cindy, and others—for the love they have given from the other side. Lastly, I thank both Heaven and Earth for the many sacred blessings I have received.

Contents

Foreword

Jillian Maas Backman is an intuitive life coach, radio personality, wife, mother of two, and friend to many. A minister's daughter who earned a degree in psychology, she has been a catalyst for change in the lives of her numerous clients. Among those she has guided are corporate executives, international business leaders, celebrity musicians, artists, authors, and school administrators. Her diverse clientele come to her seeking clarity and healing, and they often leave with an understanding of the greater meaning of their lives. These mostly professional individuals do not seem to think it strange that part of Backman's guidance is derived from messages she receives from "the other side."

A generation earlier, the search to "know thyself" or to explore one's spiritual identity was hardly mainstream. More commonly, one's relationship with God was contained within the church sanctuary. Those who dabbled in spirituality outside of religious tradition were considered fringe thinkers.

Over the past few decades, more and more people have embarked upon a less trodden spiritual path. They have opened their hearts and minds to the possibility of experiencing God in all aspects of their lives and understanding their human condition in terms of spiritual lessons to be learned. Today, many seem to be experiencing these lessons at an increased rate—modern life for many is fast-paced, challenging, and tumultuous. Concurrently, spiritual growth and knowledge is accelerated. As a way of finding guidance along this fast paced journey, information has been sought which extends beyond what has been offered by the "spiritual elite."

During this phase of spiritual evolution, the modern world is at a crossroads. Every day we are faced with an ever mounting array of natural and environmental disasters, political upheaval, social unrest, and desperate human need. At the same time, the world has become more polarized; those who seek short-term gain at the expense of the health and welfare of the planet continue on obliviously while those who would offer innovative solutions for the betterment of humanity bravely forge ahead in the opposite direction. Together, we must and will make a collective decision very soon: are we going to continue to be driven by greed and personal gain, or are we going to become more spiritually driven and consider the long term consequences of our actions?

When discussing this book with me, Backman referenced what she calls "spiritual acts of duty." She defines this term as heeding one's calling to a higher existence and living out the soul's intentions. Sometimes we discover that the work demanded of us by our souls is not what we expected, or it may seem to be more than we can bear. When seen within from the perspective of spirit, however, all of our challenges become opportunities to grow and evolve into a greater awareness of the divine presence.

It is possible to approach Backman's book as an amusing tale about a woman who converses with angels. On the other hand, *Beyond the Pews* can serve as your call to active duty in the world. It is up to you to decide.

Introduction to Using This Book

I did not set out to write an autobiography. While an account of the significant events of my childhood and life to date have in fact been shared in this book, the details of the story are not all that important. I have merely highlighted certain moments in order to illustrate how various responses and decisions changed the course of my life.

This is an "interactive biography." I have shared this personal information with you to demonstrate the impact of my choices and to encourage you to take care as you consider the choices you make in your own life. By reading this book and completing the exercises provided in the "soul lessons," you can begin to live a more awakened, spiritual life style.

For some, becoming more "spiritual" suggests that one is becoming less engaged with earthly matters, perhaps as a cloistered nun or hermetic monk. In this book you will, I hope, come to see that becoming truly spiritual means embracing the voice of your soul and carrying out the intentions of your soul in the physical world. The ambition of this book is to provide you with information and tools which will help take you further along your important sacred journey. As you awaken to the wisdom within, you will truly discover a more peaceful and fulfilling way of life.

I wish you peace, joy, and happiness as you continue traveling along your path to home.

Blessings,
Jillian

1

Do You See What I See?

I am a direct descendant of what is sometimes called "American Spiritual Royalty." This select group is comprised of preachers and their families. It's an elite subculture of individuals chosen to help God's people down the centuries'-worn trail toward human salvation. Specifically, my father was a Christian minister and I was what others tag as a "preacher's kid." This label never bothered me. In fact, I thought it was a silly slang term that described my special status. There is an odd sense of entitlement attached to this kind of illusionary notoriety. As a preacher's kid, I had direct access to the world of religious fame where privileges and opportunities abound.

My father's parish was full of successful, gracious people who were willing to share their wealth with our family in many ways. We were invited to many wonderful parties and sporting events, and we received gifts of all kinds. From a little girl's point of view, this was heavenly. Even though we were not wealthy by any standards, I felt loved by many.

It's also the case that as a preacher's family, we were held to high standards of social, physical and above all, spiritual expectations. The church, my father's career and family were one and the same. The delineation between private and public life became blurred. This environment doomed many a preacher's kid to an adult life riddled with guilt, bitterness and resentment. For some, it even led to severing ties to any religious or spiritual foundation. I was able to avoid this plight because I had something that kept me securely tethered to the edge of this dark abyss: my intuition—a God-given talent for receiving symbolic communications.

As breath gives life to my body, my intuitive sensing provides spiritual fire for my soul, Receiving faith-based sensory perceptions of all kinds.

Inspirational and soulful insights come from a world you cannot see with the naked eye. Messages are short and to the point, or lengthy and profound.

Significant teachings for myself, and ultimately for the world,

Taking months, even years to decipher.

A BEAUTIFUL SPIRITUAL BACKDROP

The ministerial profession indoctrinates its members into a nomadic existence. Children of ministers are along for the ride. Adaptability is not an option; it is a requirement. With underlying apprehension, I would settle into my temporary surroundings as best I could. My brother and I never knew when the next Godly call into new parishioner service would come.

For the most part, ministers begin their careers with a "mission parish," serving a core group of God-fearing worshipers in small villages throughout America. Whether by pre-disposed spiritual intervention or simple human luck, my father's first call into service ended up being the perfect place for me to discover the miracle of my intuitive gifts.

It was near the tail end of the "Kumbayah" era, the 1970s, with the lingering effect of 1960s idealism still filtering into the culture. For years there had been a great divide between church and politics, and it was somewhat taboo to cross into one domain from the other. But now there seemed to be a rippling in the unspoken hard lines between government policies and social concerns. During this societal shift, many sought refuge from civil unrest at their local churches. But a rise in consciousness was emerging that gave way to genuine empathy for humankind. Grasping the mood of the times, my father seized the opportunity to inspire his Christian community with this new optimism. Who knew that a quiet, unassuming church nestled tightly between the flint hills of the Missouri mountainside could transform into a congregation that would blaze a trail into the 21st century!

I remember the day we arrived in this quaint little town. Dozens of kind, loving people had been eagerly preparing for our arrival. A welcoming party of parishioners seemed full of expectations that my father, along with us, would be their beacon of light through the sea of evil. This was quite the spiritual assignment for a family of four, and especially for a shy seven-year-old girl. As a child, it was overwhelming to experience being the center of this type of attention. When grown adults treated me with grand respect and catered to my every need, I was not sure how to respond.

Our parish home was a modest three-bedroom ranch set high atop a mountainside overlooking the range. Even at my age, I knew God had brought me to a place of spectacular wonderment and magic. There was a majestic significance to the wide-open spaces where the energy was boundless and untouched by human gridlines. We settled in nicely to our daily routine. When I was not playing in my spacious backyard, I could be found at church. I found profound refuge—both physically and spiritually—inside this holy structure.

It was my job to help with the daily chores around the church. I folded bulletins for services and assisted the altar guild for Sunday morning sacraments as well as practiced with the children's choir. What others would classify as mundane church tasks were soulful assignments for me. These tasks inspired and energized me, laying the groundwork for higher gifts that were about to be received.

On Sunday mornings, my mom and I would head over to church to check in with my dad. Crossing the threshold into the sanctuary one day, I felt a jolt of electricity reverberate inside my youthful frame—a massive shock of static electricity from head to toe. It startled me and grabbed my undivided attention. I remember gazing over at my mother to see if she noticed me jump from the instantaneous incident. Nope—no reaction there. Not even a flinch. It was obvious my mother was not experiencing the same sensations. Over the course of several weeks and months, these types of occurrences became both more frequent and pronounced. Some kind of insistent "loving inward force" was vying for my attention.

I began to experience other peculiar sensations, and the intensity escalated every time I went back into church. There were days when the brightest imaginable light glowed from every crevice of the sanctuary. Transparent colors of every hue in the rainbow poured out before me. Hard surfaces, like the pews, hymnals, and particularly the altar, were gilded with a mixture of gold flecks and white flames that shone like shards of newly polished glass.

What astounded me the most were the colors encircling the people I observed. Sometimes the illumination was so bright it was unbearable to keep eye contact. My hearing was as heightened as my sense of sight. It was like a radio, picking up all the spirit channels broadcasting at once. At first, these perceptions overwhelmed me and left me feeling completely unbalanced. But it did not stop there. This invisible force tapped into every one of my five senses. The energy within would simmer like a teakettle bursting at the seams! It took everything I had to stay in that pew seat the entire length of a service. I never felt fear, though I did feel confused at times.

Is anyone else having the same experiences? I wondered. There were holograms of angels lingering in every free space imaginable. Tall ones, short ones, chubby ones. Some were just hanging around while others were speaking directly to the humans—who were oblivious to the angelic presence sitting next to them. It felt as if I were in my own little world designed only for me, though it felt entirely natural.

Yet there were times when the energy was too much for my little physique. The accumulation had to be released somehow, so I did what most normal kids do: squirmed on my pew seat. Some days this would be enough to vent the energy and some days it would not. On the days it did not, I developed a habit of jumping up and making a quick run for the restroom and finding the closest empty stall.

Then came the day when uncontrollable, scrambled language came spewing out of my mouth. Laughter in between spurts of speech helped calm the fears about what was happening to me. Later, much later, I was able to label this unconscious act: I was speaking in tongues. Even this uncommon behavior felt entirely natural to me. It was an expression of my glorious, overzealous love for God.

The part that did not make sense to me was that I did not see anyone else being moved by the brilliant energy surrounding all of us. Only a handful of folks seemed to be enjoying the celebration of God as much as I was. I was soaking up every moment of God's sunshine. Why weren't the others experiencing the "pew wiggles?" Unanswered questions started racing through my mind. What is this experience? Who is causing this to happen? What is someone trying to tell me?

Am I allowed to talk about what is occurring? Am I supposed to be experiencing these sensations?

I prided myself on being a good Christian girl. But I was aware that this kind of behavior could easily be misconstrued as an assault on the solid foundations of Christianity. Or it might be explained as a game I played to amuse myself during the long hours spent every week at church. But I was not deliberately seeking out these experiences. The angels were showing themselves to me. I had no set intention to speak in tongues in the restroom behind closed doors. These things just happened as natural occurrences.

Yet I felt as if I was peeking into places where I ought not to have been. It sometimes made me feel as though parts of me were dirty. Faithful children adhere to religious rules and regulations and remain quietly on the side. Only chosen anointed adults were allowed to serve as spiritual receivers of this kind. Obviously, I was not one of the chosen. That was my father's God-given assignment, not mine!

I was aware that there was a boundary that could not be crossed without facing consequences. Grave punishment awaited those who engaged in behavior considered by some as evil and against the written code of God. I was sometimes overwrought with fear of disapproval from both God and my minister father for breaking religious rules. The reprimands for disobedience would surely be swift from both parties, though I had no way of judging what the consequences might have been. However, my deepest sense was that nothing felt wrong or evil. Quite the contrary. A loving presence was stirring within my soul that was just as powerful as my religious convictions.

7

I soon began to feel the urge to explore "forbidden territories" and satisfy my precocious adventurous spirit. I felt enriched by my spiritual encounters and took in every message that came my way. I started to pay close attention to the details of these communications, which were often interactive parables of a sort. When a communication was received that made no sense at all, clarifying messages arrived soon thereafter. Most of the time, these communications were spiritual lessons that could only have come from outside my being. They were broad, universal thoughts and served to expand my awareness. Lessons were provided that encouraged me to question some of the very things I was being taught by adults. It was not that what I was being taught was wrong. It was that there was more to the story than I was being told.

TRANSITION TO THE "OUTSIDE WORLD"

As I grew up, these aberrational occurrences were beginning to stir up a sense of spiritual incompleteness. Gaps began to form between the knowledge taught to me by the church Elders and what my angels from the other side were tutoring. An overriding force kept pushing me down this awakened path, despite the risks. I was compelled to seek this dynamic angelic energy that existed outside my comfort zone.

I felt very much alone on this strange journey. My lifeline was the church, and there was no intrinsic reason to explore other angelic realms outside of organized religion. But now I was being sent the message to search beyond the world that was right in front of me. A sense of duality was crashing through my preconceived notions about faith. As a little kid, I did not pause to consider the meaning of the messages I was receiving from the other side. I simply reacted as the episodes happened.

My spiritual self was completely satisfied with the lessons provided. My mind, on the other hand, was begging for more information. The rational side wanted to gather up as many spiritual interactions as I could in the shortest amount of time in order to make sense of them. Eventually, I was able to reconcile my mind and spirit and strike a peaceful balance between the two sides of myself. As the same time, something else was occurring: I was co-creating a "spiritual island" off the continent from man-made religion.

I felt as though I were entering a void, of sorts.

As though I were on a bridge, half-built to another shore enriched with spiritual spoils. Propelling me to search for new tools that would construct a pathway toward something bigger than my own being. Toward everlasting internal spiritual serenity.

When the timing was right and I was ready to step into my next spiritual life lesson, all messages pointed in the direction of my own backyard, literally. When I first landed on top of the country mountain range in Missouri with my family, I remember being immediately aware that miracles would be occurring in this place. But my awareness was initially focused inside of church. My mind was preoccupied by the angelic energy and encounters I was having inside the sanctuary. Though I had been living in our parsonage home for a while,

I never really took notice of the energy in the outside world. Only after I received a specific message did I begin to realize that the energy of God could be found in my own backyard.

The energy of plants and growing things existing right outside our sliding glass doors was better known as "Mother Nature." I could hear her faint voice calling me and telling me to jump with my child feet into this world of untainted perfection. And jump in is exactly what I did! It was time to experience firsthand the energy of the earth.

I loved to walk barefoot through those flint hills. Of course, my mother and father were constantly nagging me to put on my shoes. Always being the good little girl, I would oblige and shove on the shoes just long enough to get away from eyeshot. Then off they came, regardless of the season. No difference if it was dead of winter or the scorch of the sun, I was shoeless. People always asked me why I did this. My pat answer would always be "Because it's right!"

The shoes felt constricting and were a bothersome barrier to my new physical-electric-spiritual socket. Spirit had brought forth a new energetic play toy—the energy from a different kingdom, from the wilderness. There was no way, or no one for that matter, who could stop me from downloading this power. To this day, in all my intuitive sessions, I continue to go barefoot!

No matter where I found myself physically, this intense energy would find me. Whether hiking with my dog in the woods or fishing on the lake with my family, it was beside me. I could sense a primal interdependence in the purest form. God, nature and myself. The energies surrounding me were not separate from each other; I was a quintessential ingredient in this mix of Mother Nature and God. I was like the electrical conductor that carried the current between the forces. My energy was positioned at the midpoint of the sacred triad. It was my job to regulate both forces; the power to manage the flow or current resided within me. A fair amount of time passed before I fully grasped the magnitude of this spiritual lesson. Eventually, I learned to manage these "currents" and use them to light the way on my creative journey.

I was living in a place of complete peace and quiet. I could hear my soul voice calling me to explore the mystical presence of sensory love.

Thousands of healthy trees covering the open landscape view from my backyard.

Through my soulful sensing, I could see hues of pinks, yellows, greens and blue

outlining the dense infrastructures of the leaves.

At dusk, just before the sun went down, the fading colors would hide away for the evening.

I knew that with the next sunrise, as always, my trees would inhale a great breath of intoxicating earthly scents and exhale their strong auras back into the sky,

that shallow void between branches and billowing clouds meandering by.

There was no way to predict how this unorthodox back-yard ritual would cement my long-term commitment to the primal essence with God.

Even though I was physically alone during the sunset experiences, I could sense an eerie pressure against my frame. Natural energetic forces were swirling around my entire body. It was something different from the energy I sensed in the church—that felt light, somehow top-heavy in its presentation, and unassuming. The energy from nature gave off an overpowering presence of earthly scents and heaviness... like the scent of clothes after playing in the mud. Even the holograms of nature appeared unique in their presentation. Unlike church angels, these visions were animal-like in form, strong, but peaceful. While the angelic visitors at church offered direct messages to me (much like two human beings having a conversation), the messages from nature were broader communications. They were uplifting exchanges that gently pointed the way to perpetual bliss, to time-out in silence. They showed the way to cut through human chaos and tap into what was essential to humankind: the boundless energy of the Holy Spirit.

Do You See What I See?

Holy Spirit,

Energy of God.

Nature: A virtual work of perpetual artistry,

God's subtle way of depicting the wordless relationship

Between Spirit and all humanity.

When I was too young to absorb completely the words of the Bible, I still tried to listen as best as I could to the words being spoken. I comprehended only bits and pieces, and I recited scripture here and there as well as any child could. What was starting to sink in, however, was this unconscious spiritual awareness. Even though I was too young to put into words what was going on inside of me, I could feel an unconscious "ebb and flow" pattern to these developments. There was a natural rhythm to this Godly process. This energy I was receiving was permeating into my soul and creating a second nature, fully present with God's existence. The energy allowed me to feel my way back to the original light. Eventually, I grasped the concept that we are all one complete energetic circle, designed in wordless perfection. The Holy Spirit was the force that was directing the planet's next religious quest.

With the Holy Spirit Leading the Way...

My father was notorious for shaking things up during his tenure in the ministry. There were very few boundaries he would not challenge; he sometimes took it upon himself to revise time-honored ways of doing things. He did not change things for the sake of change, however. He went about finding new solutions when he saw that old ways of doing things were no longer effective.

It is the ultimate responsibility of the minister to continuously expand the flock: i.e., to find new members. This is an especially important task for mission churches, whose survival depends on the collective tithing from church members. The incentive to find new members led both my father and other preachers to think in new directions and go where "spirit moved them." If ministers wanted to entice young people to come to church, they would have to replicate the popular cultural scene spreading through America, the hangin' in coffeehouses milieu. Places where young people could mingle, share their pop culture-style music and words of peace and harmony. In my opinion, this openness to pop culture brought the next generation to the religious communion table.

It became obvious to my father, however, that the indoor sanctuary was not a suitable place to hold these types of informal, whimsical gatherings. Without skipping a beat, my father and members of the congregation set about constructing an outdoor venue in a grassy patch behind the church proper—an outdoor sanctuary.

An altar was built and split-log seating arranged in an intimate, semi-circle within this peaceful setting. To this day, the outdoor sanctuary represents, in my mind, one of the most pure expressions of dedication to God's work here on earth. As a child, I loved this sacred, outdoor space. While other children were playing on schoolhouse playground equipment, I was playing in this sacred playground. I played leapfrog from one split-log seat to another. I sometimes served up my version of communion—squished-up white bread and grape juice in little cups "borrowed" from the altar guild room—to my angelic friends who came to play.

In this idyllic, intimate setting, the blessed forces seemed to come together in a powerful way. The energies I had originally experienced in the sanctuary and then later in my backyard were now present in full glory before me. I now knew without doubt the experiences I had had in the sanctuary were not just a fluke or isolated intuitive incidents. They were extraordinary events that would lead to a place beyond fond childhood memories. They had imprinted my being—my mind, my body, and most importantly, my spirit—with an awareness of the sacred.

I might have ignored the angelic messages, the intuitive guidance I received as a child, but this would have had a devastating effect on my psyche. Fortunately, my ego and sense of self were strong enough to allow for the possibility of an unchartered spiritual path. I have come to see that there are organic elements essential to God's plan, and I am forever humbled by this awareness. Human life progresses in a natural rhythm, which parallels the rhythms of God's own process. It is my belief that the natural rhythms of the God process are applicable to all sincere religious convictions. It is my *preference* to discuss spiritual experience from the point of view of my own origins, with the Christian voice of my childhood.

2

Soul Lessons for a Minister's Daughter

My father's assignment at the Missouri mountainside church continued until I was twelve years old. Next, our family would relocate to a large metropolitan community with a substantially larger congregation. Even though I would be leaving behind this magical, pristine, spiritual environment, my soul had been imprinted with lessons that would stay with me throughout my lifetime. It was during these years in Missouri that I began, unconsciously, to develop a permanent foundation in the unspoken aspects of spirituality—the lessons that cannot be taught with spoken words but must be experienced. The process of building this foundation begins with an instinctive spiritual innocence; while communing in the energy of God, blessings beyond the ordinary or obvious are received.

My initial introduction to this way of wakeful living was in the hill country. Every one of my physical senses was forever touched by the angelic wisdom I received from the other side. There was no denying that the intentional visitations I received had left their permanent marking on my spiritual identity. The question remained: what were these intentional encounters supposed to be teaching me?

Early on I was introduced to Christian ideology, the written word of the Bible—a compilation of refined, saintly conversations between Spirit and man that has been passed down through the ages. The common denominator of all faiths is the scribed text, whether containing the words of Jesus, Buddha, Moses, Guru Nanak or other shamans. This well-defined structure contains the spiritual recipe guiding human beings on their eternal quest for enlightenment.

Every week, as a child, I looked forward to hearing the Elders of our church orate joyful Jesus stories. There was solace in knowing that His struggles were my struggles, and that life's challenges could be spiritually overcome. Even though I was satisfied intellectually by these Sunday teachings, an internal void was starting to percolate from the inside out. The lackluster enthusiasm I sensed around others who were attending church services was beginning to spill over into my experience during Sunday school sessions. The well-meaning teachers did not know what they did not know. By no fault of their own, they were sharing with my fellow pupils an incomplete story and repeating by rote lesson plans from generations past. The experience led me to feel spiritually lopsided—like an unbalanced scale leaning too far to one side.

The Sunday school curriculum was weighed down with repetitive lessons and lacked teachings that nurtured the development of an interior, spiritual life. For instance, there were no school lesson plans on how to sense the presence of God, much less "how to chat with the angels." Because this was not discussed, I refrained from "childhood chatter" about my experiences with the other kids. I did not feel free to swap ideas on how not to be caught playing an invisible game of hide and seek with spiritual visitors during church service. I was never able to talk about what God "feels like" inside my body. In my own mind, I referred to this sensation as my "tingles from head to toe."

No one at church ever discussed communicating with animals or receiving messages from spirits. But I knew instinctively, without being told by grown-ups, that both the standard religious teachings and the intuitive sensing I was experiencing came from the same source. Both were derived from the spark that keeps the flames roaring in human souls—the source of God. Though I was aware of this sacred presence within us all, others did not seem to speak of it. The apparent absence of awareness led me to another lingering question that remains unanswered to this day: Was I the only one within the entire congregation who was experiencing these angelic visitations and this infinite wordless wisdom?

Every little kid thrives on adult confirmation or approval for spiritual devotion. It is one of the stable building blocks upon which all religions build. Mine never came. However, I did receive approval from one significant place—the only place that truly mattered. The approval came from my loving spiritual teachers from another plane, my appointed overseers who would stay with me for the rest of my time on earth.

Though I could not put my finger on it, I could sense that something was not right as I was growing up in my father's church. My "angelic friends" provided an answer of sorts. As children, we all start with similar opportunities to sense invisible energy and commune with spirits from the other plane, to explore the phenomenon of the inner working of our universe. To remain grounded on this planet, however, it is necessary to maintain balanced, synchronized rhythms between the two dominant energetic forces: polarities known in the religious world as Heaven and Earth. Each one houses distinct characteristics.

The first polarity is the "essence of Heaven." Many sacred texts refer to it as the ultimate holy gift from above. It is unreasonable to assume that you can totally experience heavenly feelings inside a living human body. However, there are techniques that can replicate the feeling of Holy Spirit within. This modest energy trail usually begins at the top of the head and permeates the body quickly. The energy is very light in its presentation. In addition, if you are not paying attention, you can lose the connection within a minute or two. It was this kind of energy I felt initially inside my father's church. This particular energy reminds us of why we are truly here: to rise above our earthly desires and seek eternal life.

The second polarity is the "energy of Earth." Though this energy is not described in all religious texts, it is just as powerful in keeping human beings balanced. This energy has a greater density when it resonates throughout the body. It literally feels like you have rocks in your pocket. Heavy by design, it enters the body through the feet and travels slowly upward toward the top of the head. This Earth energy is responsible for keeping one grounded in the present moment. It encourages humankind to honor the planet and reminds us that we are interconnected.

All living creatures carry both essential life forces within their physical structures. The soul center of the human acts as the great spiritual navigator of these two energy forces. The soul center is the centralized location whereby both energies intersect. It is the tireless workhorse constantly nudging humanity toward its heavenly mission of traveling beyond religious limitations and enjoying the spiritual wave of illumination.

Like a human fingerprint, every soul vibrates to its own energetic eccentricities. These eccentricities comprise an internal moral compass, superseding all others. They direct each of us to an awareness of the "energetic fire" of choice. Inside each one of us is a personal "Eden," or a world filled to the brim with organic truths that we have the opportunity to embody if we so choose. This fertile ground is what leads the masses toward religious compassion, forgiveness and, above all, love. No matter what religious underpinning is held sacred, each of us has the ability to feel the God source within ourselves and more importantly, in others.

As childhood leads to adolescence, human life passes through an individualized, spiritual evolution. During this unwritten rite of passage, one arrives at a secular fork in the road. At this juncture, organized religion has the potential to "overseed" natural intuition, what I call the language of "spiritual intuitive sensing." This is the place where the intricate balance between heavenly and earthly energies can be accidentally thrown off. Religious logic can often overpower the more ethereal, energetic feelings. When this occurs, soul intentions are often abandoned while spiritual innocence is forgotten.

This rite of passage became ever so poignant as I experienced a moment of spiritual awakening on the hillside when I was growing up. I was alone on my journey, accompanied only by my soulful, spiritual bliss. It was a point in time when I felt in complete harmony with the energies of God, nature and the spirituality of all humankind. It was the internal ecstasy that can only come when you allow yourself to be in complete surrender to all of God's impeccable creations. In this place, I felt as if the Holy Spirit was standing right beside me, a dove descended on rays of light.

The experience was like receiving a healing and resembled an electric pulse mimicking the vibrations of a ticking heartbeat and radiating out in an enormous circumference. I felt no human mistrust as this occurred, only the indisputable presence of the Holy Spirit, the Holy Ghost of Christianity, guiding my way. My entire being was in absolute alignment with all that the God source had meticulously designed. Inside my being, something "clicked," and I realized that both my spiritual intuitive language and my chosen religion were necessary to maintain a stable and healthy spiritual life. Both sources of knowledge instilled an undying allegiance to my faith.

While I was developing this unique spiritual foundation,

most other children were unconsciously letting go of their soul-sensing ability and veering onto well-worn, intellectual paths of religious expression. I was headed down a road less traveled and was given the grace to maneuver through this transitional time with my untainted connection to Spirit intact. Somehow, I learned to navigate successfully in the world without abandoning either the heavenly or earthly training. I was given the courage to be different and act upon the unsolicited advice from the ones who love me the most: my watchful invisible guardians.

Both the steady stream of inspiring messages from the other side and my unwavering association with the church gave me the conviction to follow my special path in life. While other children were content with their more traditional religious teachings, I was being shown unique problem-solving techniques while tucked away in my own private sanctuary. For every religious lesson I would receive in Sunday school, the angels would complete the circle with practical wisdom. I understand this might seem counterintuitive to the way it should be. After all, why would anyone label communication with other side as *practical wisdom*? However, I believe that angelic energies from the other side are meant to enhance the experience of religious text. They give voice to silent, unspoken words.

This was the way it came to pass with the interactions and information from my angelic posse. It was as if they were leading me to peek in the darkened corners of a room in order to illuminate knowledge forgotten by the rest of the world. They constantly encouraged me to ask important questions about information being omitted from the religious material being taught. In this way, the foundations were laid for what I call my "spiritual clearing house techniques." The set of religious and spiritual criteria that evolved out of these techniques shaped the pluralistic servant that I am today.

3

First Soul Lesson

Experiencing God

Though the lessons taught to us by Jesus and other spiritual teachers are often beautifully simple in their truth, modern Western religion is often fraught with complications and disagreements over how to practice our faith or which faith is best. Additionally, we have convinced ourselves that participating in religious or spiritual activity is labor-intensive. Some spend countless hours memorizing written passages. Others seem to await patiently the opportune moment to defend with conviction the tenets of their faith to those lost souls who simply do not comprehend. Sometimes religious activity is devoted to rote rituals while "feelings of the Lord" are cast aside. When this happens, the energy of God and the lessons that are naturally imparted from this personal connection become an entirely separate category of faith.

I am not sure of the origins of this unfortunate separation of natural spiritual experience and religious faith. Perhaps it resulted from unfounded fears of the unknown or from misinterpretation. There may have been a notion long ago that worshipers would naturally assimilate the feelings of God as they listened to scripture. Or the dominance of the intellectual path might have been a by-product of studying religious text over time. Another explanation is that the innate, childlike awareness of God simply fades away due to lack of use. Regardless, many choose a path of intellectual certainty and abandon the more unpredictable, intuitive course.

The lessons derived from our innate experience with God shape our spiritual character just as our traditional lessons and liturgy do. We often forget the significance of the natural spiritual connection because of its subtleties. Interweaving practical knowledge without notice, Mother Nature is neither boastful nor flamboyant in presentation. Her lessons have not been recorded in a published text. There is no scripture to draw from or insight to be taught each week. The lessons simply arise from everyday human activities. When the connection to our innate spiritual wisdom is lost, spiritual innocence is simultaneously forgotten.

Neither the traditional nor the natural course is wrong to follow. There is no benefit in choosing just one over the other. The truth of the matter is that the paths are not mutually exclusive, and one should not replace the other. In fact, by assimilating wonders from both dualities, rich and lasting rewards are gained.

The promising news is that your spiritual intuitive language will be sending signals and guiding you to a place of spiritual equilibrium throughout your lifetime. The messages subtly remind you to return to your energetic home base, where all spiritual energy resides—the human soul. The connection between your intuitive nature and your soul never truly disintegrates; it simply lies dormant, waiting patiently for your triumphant return.

I embrace the gifts of living in spiritual innocence,
with the reassurance that my faith is a reflection of
both Heaven and Earth.

My human soul—the organic element—holds this
sacredness within me,
where both Heaven and Earth reside eternally,
side-by-side.

Numerous benefits are achieved when the original balance of the energy of God is recreated within your being. Many find that calm and peacefulness are acquired by restoring the innate spiritual rhythm to its original blueprint. Personally, I have found that spiritual patience—a quality that allows you and those you interact with the space and time to obtain ultimate harmony—to be one of the most profound rewards. Sacred timing—when events occur at the most opportune time—is another blessing.

While experiencing the angelic interactions inside my father's church or outside in my backyard, I had no way of physically manipulating these visitations or willing them to be. I was simply open and receptive to the events as they appeared to me—much as I am now. I have no personal stake in seeking out my angelic lessons from the other side. I live day-to-day with the underlying acceptance and confidence that I receive what I am intended to receive. This allows me the luxury of living in the moment. I have the assurance that if a new lesson is necessary, it will be presented in a pointed way, so that I hear or see what is intended.

TOP HEAVY VERSUS BOTTOM HEAVY

The first soul lesson I offer to you is simple yet profound. In the following exercise, you will take an honest assessment of your own patterns of experiencing God. You will identify your tendency to experience either intellectually or intuitively.

It is very easy to lose ourselves in the intellectual abyss we have often diligently constructed. This is especially true in the realm of our religious life. When this occurs, we become "bottom heavy," or excessively immersed in physical, earthly matters. At the same time, we forget to embrace the spiritual powers from the heavenly forces of the world. This includes angelic messages, religious prayer, the communion of saints or other forms of contact.

On the other hand, the opposite can occur. Some become too "top heavy" and spend the majority of time "out in the heavens." When this happens, people are not fully present with the earthly tasks directly in front of them. They seek out experiences of spiritual bliss while sometimes dismissing time-honored spiritual traditions or forgetting the physical work that needs to be accomplished in the world.

The goal of this first assignment is to get to know your tendencies and to understand all facets of your earthly self and your heavenly self. From there, you can let your soul center be your guide.

Refrain from making this first lesson too complicated, neither should you label this as a childish task. Do not allow your religious knowledge to be your "spirit roadblock" to success. While the lesson may seem a simple one, it may take several tries for you to become aware of your spiritual rhythm system and to break the pattern.

EXERCISE ONE: DISCOVERING YOUR SPIRITUAL RHYTHM

Which energetic style best represents the way you process the world you live in right now? Are you "bottom heavy?" The spiritual dynamics in your life are well defined when you are bottom heavy. You have a tendency to see everything from more of a structured religious vantage point. You might think, "If it is not written in my sacred text, it isn't real."

Alternatively, are you "top heavy?" Are you free-thinking when it comes to spirituality? Perhaps you understand there is some kind of higher power but your interpretation of God is loosely defined. You believe everyone has the right to express their faith as they choose. You believe what matters more than a specific religion is your own interpretation of faith.

Establish in your mind those statements that best

represent your own belief system. Start by going back in your memory bank and recalling your precious early days of Sunday school or your first spiritual experiences connected with your chosen religious and spiritual path. See if you can reclaim within yourself the feelings of uncensored innocence—the kind of feelings associated with a childhood religious song, church play or even a religious story from a cherished chapter.

Since I was a youngster, my favorite song has always been *Amazing Grace*. When I was a little girl, it felt as if the song was being sung just for me, and my body trembled with joy for being so special in the eyes of God. Words came alive with vibration from every translated lyric, and faith was stripped down to its most simple, honest form. Once you have experienced the energy of higher grace, the knowledge of it belongs to you forever. However, many adults have left the memory of it behind years ago. Has time robbed you of your own spiritual innocence? Are you so bottom heavy in your religious convictions there is no room for your own soulful voice to find its way into your daily routine? Have you drifted too far away from the free-spirit side of the natural rhythm and are you now struggling to reclaim this part of yourself?

On the other hand, are you on the opposite side—too top heavy? Have you followed such a nebulous path of spiritual expression that you have abandoned the sense of religious foundations that keeps human beings focused on the common unity of our earthly existence? Do you move from one tradition to another without establishing a regular spiritual practice? Have you immersed yourself in spiritual books, the New Age movement or religious thought but lost your connection to a wider community of faith?

Now you can begin to identify what actions you can take to reinstate that natural energy flow between the energy of God, your soul self and Earth. Figure one illustrates this energy pattern.

FIGURE ONE

Sometimes it is difficult to achieve a balance between the energies, and I must admit that I sometimes veer from one extreme to the other. There are days when I find myself so top heavy that I feel like I could topple over any second with the abundance of spiritual visions dancing in my head. Then there are weeks when I am so engrossed in earthly concerns that I lose countless hours of good sleep. I have devoted my life to communing with and loving both parts of this experience. However, I become immobilized if I allow myself the luxury of staying too long in either dimension. When this starts to happen, I take measures to regain my equilibrium.

When feeling bottom heavy, I deliberately grant myself an intellectual time-out and let my soul be the forerunner to spiritual resuscitation. One of my favorite pastimes is attending meditative services on a regular basis. This in itself is not a spectacular event; we all have experienced some kind of meditative practice. Here is the part that separates my meditative state from many others: the services I attend are not performed in English. Moreover, I do not comprehend the language they are speaking at these services. Words become insignificant. In fact, they become cumbersome to the process. When you are taken out of your normal religious rituals, something interesting occurs. You begin to rely heavily upon your own intuitive, spiritual feelings.

I participate in this unusual type of service in order to remind myself of the precious awakening I received all those years ago: the innocent, universal language of spiritual love. It is a world beyond any pews, outdoor sanctuaries or even my backyard playground. It is a place filled with the quiet, energetic wonderment of heaven, earth and the center of my soul. If we have been spiritually dormant for a while, it takes effort to achieve an awakened state of awareness. Give yourself permission to feel the essence of childlike spiritual presence in your life again.

Exercise 2: Sensing the Energy of God

Next, I invite you to find a quiet and calm place in your home, away from outside distractions. Close your eyes and ask yourself what the energy of God feels like inside your own physical being. Afford yourself the opportunity to sense without spiritual boundaries. For me, this includes gently releasing words or language from my mind. Feel your way through this exercise. What are you sensing inside your own soul center? Make note of every little sensation. Sometimes the most subtle indicator will guide you back into a natural spiritual rhythm.

Achieving a balanced energy pattern is one of the spiritual foundations necessary in keeping sacred religious convictions intact. Through the silent language of spiritual intuitive sensing, you will learn to keep your soul, intellect, and intuition in equilibrium and working energetic order.

4

A Devastating Loss

The conversations that occurred between my angelic friends and me started out as innocent childhood amusement. My communications with these otherworldly beings were a way of keeping my youthful, inquisitive self entertained during the long hours spent in church. As time went on, I learned to trust these visitors from the other side and to gain confidence in the information they imparted to me. These unique relationships became naturally incorporated into my life while I continued to maintain the religious practice that I also cherished.

When I was a young child, communications with the other side were one way; I was always on the receiving end of the dialogue. The messages were light-hearted and provided reassurance of the goodness and loving nature of God. Giggles were certainly permitted and even encouraged by my spiritual teachers when we "talked." The thought never crossed my mind there was some sort of higher plan to the unorthodox lessons I was receiving. But in fact, this early instruction served an important purpose; it provided the internal subflooring for the spiritual housing that was being built within me.

The teachings I learned from church and those received directly from the spiritual realm were not contradictory in my mind. Through these two sources of wisdom, I was assimilating an awareness of both heavenly and earthly energetic rhythms. Through the sacred language of intuitive sensing, I was able to achieve a healthy balance between my innate spiritual innocence and organized religion. An important lesson that was to follow these conversations waited patiently around the corner.

It was soon time for me to leave spiritual kindergarten and graduate into the human school of hard knocks. Before I knew what was happening, the curriculum changed and the lessons I learned were not just for fun any more. In the frequently harsh world of reality, my spiritual intuitive sensing would serve as the compass leading the way.

As a minister's daughter, a cast of thousands appeared in the play that was my life. Some were passing through only for a short time, while others became lifelong friends. As people came and went from the parish, I was exposed to many adult challenges. The toughest of these was dealing with the stark reality of death—a difficult subject to handle, even for grown-ups. Within the congregation at any given time, there was always someone passing over.

It was my father's responsibility to guide the loved ones left behind through their traumatic hardships. These weighty obligations left him with little time and patience to deal with my less pressing concerns. For the most part, I was left to my own devices when it came to coping with death and dying. In an effort to understand the process of death, I assumed the role of my own in-home schoolteacher and made use of every available religious and spiritual resource to tackle the challenge. Like a Ping-Pong ball, I bounced back and forth between human and heavenly classrooms, trying to make sense of the transitions I witnessed.

It was during one of these lessons when I came to realize that I was blessed with two sets of parents: my human parents, who were assigned with the earthly task of instructing me on religious doctrine, and a set of angelic parents (guardian angels, if you will), who were responsible for helping my awakened soul to thrive. I am quite aware that this kind of bond is unconventional by normal standards. Though it sometimes required effort to keep these sacred relationships intact, this unique arrangement allowed me to experience life in reverse order: spiritual experiences first, physical experiences second. To this day, I continue to experience life in this way.

My guardian angels were present with me one day when I stopped to ask a specific question about a woman who was sitting in my father's church. An older woman, she was extremely dedicated to the church's mission. Over the course of the next few Sundays, my attention continued to be directed toward her, perhaps because of my spiritual talent for observing the elusive colors that surround people and objects. I was able to detect a change in the color palette surrounding this parishioner. The spheres of bright red that usually encircled her silhouette were fading into the background. The red color was giving way to a muted haze of white mist that was making its way closer and closer to her perimeter. I wanted to know what the changing colors signified.

It also appeared that this woman's vivacious personality was slowly dissolving right before my eyes. In its place emerged a strange, unassuming essence of calmness. I felt curious about this change I was witnessing. I had seen the white mist around other people before, but never to this dramatic degree. Despite my curiosity, part of me was hesitant to go near her; I didn't want the white haze to attach to me for some reason. Even from a distance, I could sense that she was becoming more spiritual than human.

The purity resonating from the woman's body was intoxicating. It was a spiritual perfume like no other, with sweet notes mixed with the essences of distinct heavenly blessings: harmony, serenity, power and completion. If I was attentive in her presence, I could also detect the discrete but supportive undertones of all religious thoughts: trust, truth and the sacred promise of a new spiritual dimensional beginning. I knew the white haze surrounding her was a mystery of some special significance. Soon the white color overshadowed the red. Some time after the red color completely disappeared, the woman died.

Immediately after her death, I was struck by a realization: I had posed a question in my mind and received an answer from my guardian angels in return. It was a change from the one-sided interactions I'd had before with the other side. My intuitive language was stretching the human ground rules once again as I headed into uncharted territory. I had been grappling alone with the limited knowledge and vocabulary of a child as I observed the dying woman in church. The answer I was seeking required wisdom that extended beyond my limited scope of knowledge. But the minute this question became known to the spirit world, an answer followed. It was very much like two humans having a conversation.

However, this particular conversation was not ordinary; it was void of spoken words. Rather, it was an intuitive exchange between my soul and my attentive guides from another plane. The spiritual answers I received were scripted in symbolic language that I was able to decode. I had inadvertently tapped into the Rosetta Stone that translated heavenly guidance for earthly events. This universal language links the unconscious mind with our human forms.

Somewhere deep within I knew all along what was happening to the woman when the colors surrounding her began to change. The white glow signified her passing from this world to the next. At this point in time, my intellectual understanding was finally catching up with my soul development, and I felt compelled to connect human experiences to their spiritual counterparts. My guardian angels helped me understand the human loss I witnessed in terms of spiritual truth. This was wisdom I would learn to rely on again and again during moments of uncertainty. It would carry me through both good times and bad times of the human journey.

Lord ~

**Grant me the infinite foresight to keep my abstract
intuitive communication open**

**and the human courage to stay bound in truthful
servitude to this insightful gift forever.**

The next lesson on my personal journey would test everything I had learned thus far and would challenge at the core the commitment I had made to intuitive language. Either the vulnerable bond would be severed forever *or* the bond would strengthen and I would continue in the same direction with spiritual angels guiding my way.

During my early years, I experienced more significant losses than the average child. These types of experiences create an imprint upon your soul and stay with you for a very long time. Each friend who passed made a deep impression on my soul. Each loss also served to bring me to a state of greater awareness. To the outside world, I dealt with the experience of death much like everyone else. What was unknown to others was the way I handled it internally. Hidden within my intuitive world, I retreated in order to care for my worldly wounds with ethereal bandages to help the pain go away. Not a day goes by that I do not thank God for granting me the privilege of experiencing these losses. Later, I would desperately need the lessons I had learned during these times in order to survive. They would be my rescue net when I tripped and fell into a deathly, human pothole.

As a young girl, my bedroom was my sacred sanctuary providing respite from the constant firestorm of activity that surrounded me. It was an expansive gateway to realities beyond. I treasured every minute alone in this protective shelter. Here, I could examine what I had learned from my experiences in church about tapping into the energy from the other side. Soon I discovered that I could replicate these experiences whenever I wanted. Conversations with my angelic guides flowed with abandon. Whenever I needed unbiased spiritual guidance, I would simply turn soulfully inward. The key to all of it was patience. When the time was right for the answer, it would simply present itself. I discovered that "spiritual timing" was something I could depend upon. In the humble surroundings of my little room, I felt at peace.

But one fateful day, the security of my childhood clubhouse was violated by the harsh reality of human frailty. I had been playing alone quietly in my pink, girly bedroom and listening to my one-speaker, AM alarm clock radio. Happily removed from all outside intrusions, I escaped into my world of private thoughts while dancing trancelike to the funky tunes of the day. Then, in a life-altering moment, I was abruptly body-slammed back into real-time.

In the middle of a song, an ominous voice—a male disc jockey—broke through to announce a special report. Immediately I froze, listening. A child had been killed earlier that day; she had been hit by a car. Then the voice reported the name of the little girl. It was a name I recognized. She was one of my closest friends from school.

Grief does not adequately describe what I felt at that moment. My body went on autopilot as numbness began to set in. For a time, I was in a holding pattern and had no idea what to do next. Then the natural emotions that everyone suffers in these situations came rushing at me from all directions: confusion, anger, dismay and denial. I felt particularly furious with one particular source: my angelic friends from the other side. Where had they been when this was happening?

My religious teachings set forth that God and all the sacred powers that be were in charge of this world. I would have attested to this fact up until then. My angelic friends had been with me on my journey every step of the way up to that point. At this painful juncture, however, it did not feel as though anyone was present with my friend or me. The experience was completely unlike any of the self-taught, intuitive games I'd played in the past. More than this, there seemed to be no logic in this situation.

In the past, the spiritual language of colors encircling human forms had provided fair warning when death was approaching—as in the case of the older woman surrounded by the white mist at church. She had led a fruitful journey and was probably ready for new beginnings of a special kind. A natural transition had occurred, and the gift of eternal life hereafter was timely. Even though her passing was sorrowful, it was not an event that was questioned. This experience of death was one that I had been able to accept.

The sudden passing of my friend who was my own age, however, was not right. It never dawned on me that death might visit the young, the healthy or the strong. Something went terribly wrong here. There had been no warning signs from my angelic friends, and I was struck by the unfairness of it. Drowning in a cesspool of denial, I begged for swift intervention from the other side. At very least I wanted some kind of spiritual justification for this terrible tragedy, which had struck too close to home. As I waited, the silence was paralyzing and left me gasping for air.

For several years I had been building trustworthy connections with my angelic friends. Many insights had been gained, but in the face of this sudden tragedy, I quickly pronounced these relationships worthless. The ethereal visitors had tried to lure a poor child into some sort of deceptive game. If we were all on this journey together, then where were my angelic guides now? Nowhere to be found, apparently. For a few agonizing moments, the pain and sense of abandonment was excruciatingly raw.

Many years later, it's easier to make sense of what was going on inside my little head at the time. After the adrenaline kicked in, the surge of energy I felt served to fuel the pain and had me pacing back and forth across the floor countless times. Finally exhausted, I fell into a heap onto the carpeted floor. My little frame just crumpled up into a powerless ball of anguish. I'm not sure how long I remained in that position, though in my child's mind, it seemed like eternity. Each second passed in slow motion.

At last, despite delusional fog, I managed to pull myself up and make my way towards the door to find my mom. Then, like a lightning strike, an unseen force took over the room. By this time in my life, I was experienced enough in sensing spiritual energy that I could tell I was no longer alone. Through the deathly silence, I heard a firm but loving message loud and clear: *Stay put.*

I remember being completely startled by the impact of this swirling, powerful force of energy. There was no lighthearted kidding around this time; I was afraid of both the message and the formidable messenger. I understood that a critical decision had to be made: I could stay with my intuitive guidance or I could walk away from it.

If I stayed, I knew it would be embarking on a spiritual journey from which there was no returning. And it would be something more than the happy angelic dialogues of the past. This new messenger had been sent by a higher power to test me and the spiritual connection that had been forged. Trapped in my room with my relentless spirit teachers, I faced a crucial choice as well as the inescapable fact that my dearest friend had now cycled back from this plane to another. I could either escape through the door in front of me, or I could stay put, as instructed.

I shudder to think about the turn my life would have taken if I had allowed myself to fail this test. Surrendering my heart, I stayed in the room with my teachers. Losing my friend was devastating enough; losing my connection to the God source would have been inconceivable.

Once the decision was made, chaos melted into calm. Intuitively, I knew I had made the right decision. As I centered myself in the middle on the floor between the bed and the window, I finally sensed the energy that had been there through the entire episode. In fact, I could sense not one presence, but dozens who had come to comfort me in this time of acute need. Soft, muted but unfamiliar symphonic tones filled my ears, returning my tense body to a meditative state of awareness. The composition was like nothing I had ever heard before; it had been written in the heavens. Most tunes have a clearly defined melodic separation between the various instruments. In this unique piece, all the instruments resounded at once. Harps supplied the bottom notes for grounding; flutes supplied the higher notes to encourage a strong connection to the heavens. The notes in between were meant to replicate the unique pitch of my own soul.

Though I was calming down, my intuitive sensing reminded me to stay on guard and remain alert to the next wave of unstable feelings bubbling to the surface. Sure enough, my mind returned to my departed friend again. Questions that demanded answers came roaring out. I wanted an explanation from the other side about where my friend went. Why did this happen to her? I demanded. Was she in pain? Is she safe, now?

I implored my spirit guides to help me make sense of her departure. I asked to be rescued from the faithless confusion still surrounding me. Long, ethereal conversations ensued between my guardian angels and me that day. The religious and spiritual questions that came up as a result of this tragic accident were addressed. Question after question was answered as I listened with alertness, taking in every intuitive message they were sharing. Finally I reached a point of understanding.

The spirit voices spoke of heaven and the walk every human being must take in order to receive the blessings in the end. I came to understand that there is a higher plan for each life that walks this planet. My friend was a part of this plan, also known as the cycle of life. Somewhat accepting of the fact my dearest pal had passed and was never coming back, I was coming to see the relevance of this experience. Finally able to accept the essence of peace I was given, I felt cradled in the familiar hand of God.

I wish I could have stayed in this suspended state of grace forever. It would have been immeasurably preferable to what was coming next. When I finally left my room and walked out the door, my ability to survive the turmoil that followed would prove to be a testament to my intuitive foundation.

5

Lessons on Dying

After hearing the tragic news of my friend's death, I remained in the comforting presence of my spirit guides for some time. Hidden in my bedroom, I prepared for the challenge I would meet outside the door.

Even when death is anticipated, it is never a pleasant subject to discuss. We have all experienced some form of loss, for it is impossible to escape the reality of the human life cycle. Facing our personal tragedies, we are compelled to examine all aspects of mortality. Though it seems unfair, death does not always discriminate based on age.

It is my belief that each life that passes away from us creates an imprint on the unconscious mind and provides a glimpse of the higher mystery that lies behind our day-to-day experience. It is possible to tap into this wealth of spiritual wisdom if you are willing to search deep enough. Alternatively, if you are willing to take a giant step back and look down at your life from far above, the entire experience can be viewed from the larger perspective of spirit.

When I first heard the news of my friend's death broadcast on the radio, I became broken, suffering with soul-aching disbelief. Secluded alone in my bedroom, at first I was too paralyzed with anxiety to reach out to anyone for help. I felt trapped in a no-man's land between heaven and earth, as though searching to find my lost friend. My mind wandered in a desert filled with useless doubts and fears.

As I remained in my room, I received some solace from the religious beliefs that I held in high reverence. What I had been taught in church and Sunday school temporarily quieted my mind and body, but this knowledge did not soothe the deep sorrow in my soul. The support offered to me by my faith just did not seem sufficient. As I continued to drown in my pain, I unknowingly turned my back on any spiritual or religious consolation. I began to buy into the illusion that my beliefs were, at best, useless theories not to be trusted.

I yearned to find a way to make sense of what was happening, to find a solid foundation upon which I could move forward from this place of despair. What I needed was a belief system that would encompass all of my past spiritual experiences, every angelic insight from the other side, every Bible story, sermon and religious conversation I had ever had with my parents and friends. However, it was not there. All I could find were fractured, isolated incidents and verbiage with no cohesive glue holding them together. Perhaps this sounds like a naive explanation to a complex esoteric issue, but this was my raw state of mind at the time.

Slowly, I began to grasp the spiritual assignment that I was being dealt that day. It was a daunting task placed upon my small shoulders, but somehow I was supposed to move to a place of higher understanding. Through the experience of my loss, I would find my way into the belief system itself and become the human moderator, or interpreter. I needed to widen my spiritual scope to include every insightful nugget of information before me. When all the hundreds and thousands of pieces were assembled in order, I would find an all-encompassing spiritual paradigm. Years later, my words and actions would become a reflection of this new worldview.

We all come to a crisis of faith at some point in our lives, though we never really know when this will occur. Age has absolutely nothing to do with it. My "time" just so happened to come earlier rather than later in life. Faced with the devastating loss of my friend, I had no choice but to work through this predicament and battle through the confusion and darkness until I reached the daybreak of spiritual acceptance.

The process of reconciliation began as my guides began to speak to me. Following an initial period of hysteria, when I calmed down, I was at last ready to listen to the "angelic pep talk." All human distractions were put on hold, and I became ready to absorb every syllable. With the reassuring knowledge the angelic guides would not leave my side, I began to let go of all preconceived notions.

My body, literally, felt light as a feather—less like living flesh and more like pure energy. It felt as if I had my own set of wings that would allow me to fly away and escape the drama unfolding below. I began to sense what my guides were sensing. Even my breath was in sync with their breath. In and out, in and out. I knew that my guardian angels had finally arrived to lend their heavenly voice to this human tragedy.

You might have thought that the discussion with my guides would have focused on my friend's premature death and her transition to the heavenly realm. While there were momentary references to her safe eternal travels, the focus of the talk was on the continued connection I would have with her even after her departure. I was taught how to celebrate her essence as I lived my own life journey. Her spiritual legacy was forever imprinted on my soul. Beyond the bedroom door, there would be many complex, human issues to face. As I listened to my spirit guides, however, I learned ways to "stroll" through all the difficulties that lay ahead.

Sitting cross-legged on the floor in my bedroom, I remained focused on the energies surrounding me. I sensed many of us joined together in that tiny space. On either side of me were my guardian angels, who were covering my hands with their hands. Their communications were coming gently across now; in essence, they were telling me everything would be all right.

I can still recall the details of this intimate conversation. The memory of that day is seared in my mind—it was the day in which my spiritual ideology forever changed. Though this incident happened many years ago, I vividly remember how my guides began to speak to me.

Initially, they were shifting my attention back to my religious convictions. This was necessary because my doubts and uncertainties were getting in the way of the healing that I so desperately needed. They must have sensed my hesitation to follow the message as they provided these reassuring words:

"Your suffering has summoned our assistance. We are here to keep you safe! We want to share insights that will help you understand the higher meanings behind the cycle of life and death.

"It is hard to figure out why your friend has become a human angel. No one can predict when these kind of tragic moments happen. Sometimes they come without notice. The best anyone can do is simply accept this fate and try to find meaning in the middle of the chaos. Listen as best you can to the words we share. We know that you will not understand or comprehend all of the information. Know it will make more sense to you as you grow older. We trust you can do this. We know your spirit. It can handle lessons beyond your physical limitations.

"First and foremost, know that we have no heavenly intentions to ask you to give up on your religious rites. Embrace these teachings forthrightly to mend your broken heart. Fill your mind with as many Bible stories as you can. Welcome your parents, the church and the members into your inner circle of grief. Share in the healing process together so you all may move from your present place of sorrow and end in greater hopes of tomorrow. We shall be there with you at all times. Working side-by-side in tandem with your church family until all of you obtain peace once again."

The message was loud and clear: Stay with what you know best in this situation. In other words, remain connected with my religion. I was given the signal that I should release myself from my sequestered spot and return to my community, but for the time being I remained mesmerized by spirit and just sat there motionless. My teachers were far from finished with this angelic classroom session. From here on out, the uncommon conversation was filled with insights that soared way above my young head.

Throughout this unplanned meeting, my guides spoke one mantra repeatedly. Though I have no idea how many angels in all were in attendance with me on that fateful day, I was aware that they were chanting one particular statement in unison. It sounded like a serenade of hundreds of voices:

"You will forever remember every feeling, every sensation, every word we share in these moments together."

I remember thinking to myself how annoying this refrain was becoming. It played in my head like a broken record of my spiritual parents' voices. However, this mantra has remained imprinted in my memory to this day.

Before sitting down with my angelic guides, my mind was a jumbled mess extending in all directions, and my emotions were flowing unbridled. As I continued to sit with the angels, however, I began to find relief in the knowledge that my friend was being cared for spiritually. My focus turned inward, toward my own suffering. I would somehow have to live with the indisputable fact that my friend would not be coming over to play any more. No more overnights in sleeping bags and late-night TV. What could my guardian angels say that would soothe my tortured soul?

I cried and cried, my tears like drops of fire searing holes in my life force, weakening me. The more tears I shed, the more I resisted the difficult message telling me to walk straight into the open pit before me. My angelic guidance was prompting me to fight through the emotions and delve deeper into the middle of this unchartered pain. I was supposed to relinquish my familiar zone of safety and travel into an unknown world where healing could take place. It is a place that most of us are too fearful to explore. With trepidation, I finally agreed to embark on this journey.

The message I received was to connect to the untainted soul. The soul is the point of intersection within your being where earthbound religion and heavenly abstractions meet and resonate in tune with one another. Often accessed during periods of intense desperation and human defeat, it is the place where all mystical, multidimensional wisdom is revered. It was where I could find the honest, unfiltered truth about the transformation that occurs after death—the answers I was seeking. With attention focused on my heart, I continued to listen to my angelic guides.

"We see the cycle of life and death differently than you. Your friend will not be with you any more, but will be with you always in spirit. You can talk with her any time you wish. Your soul voice to her spirit voice. And she with you, her spirit voice to your soul voice. In the same fashion, we have been speaking with you in the past. These communications will assist with your healing—from the inside out, from your soul center.

"The soul is where God's energy resides within you. It will never leave you, abandon you, or betray you. Nor can anyone ever steal this energy away from you. This is where you will find your friend's energy as well. Together, they will guide you through this. No matter what comes your way, turn your face upward and know we are there.

"You own the intuitive tools to stay connected with us. Use them wisely. At all times your soul will hold the essence of your friend close, through your five senses: vision, hearing, taste, touch and smell. When you need comfort from the evils in the world, know her angel energy will come to you as fast as possible. You will know she has arrived when you energetically hear the unmistakable symphonic sounds echoing in your ears from this day forward. In the same way, the scent of the older woman's perfume will linger every so often to alert you that someone is close to going to their heavenly home.

"We also wish to tell you that there are hidden mysteries

behind the ability to see colors. Many hold the same ability to see color formations around others. Unlike you, many will be too afraid to use it. Too fearful to see the truth in the world they live in. Trust what you are shown. Let your actions speak for your visions. Above all, respect and honor your God-gifted intuitive nature. Do not abuse it for any reason. It will bring you joy beyond your wildest dreams. Hold tight to what you are sensing when the outside world tells you something different. Reach for this higher wisdom from now on in every moment of your life. Let no one take your love-essence of life, even in the midst of sorrowful death.

"Close your eyes and use your imagination to sense what we are sending your way. Your friend did not return home to punish herself or to punish you for something you did or said. Neither one of you did anything wrong. This is simply the plan of life and death on the planet. Please take time to embrace every emotion you are feeling right now. We want you to heal your mind, body and spirit. Every emotion has purpose. Feelings of anger, sadness, disappointment and fear are there to help your mind express this loss. Your body will cry real tears. The soul heals itself differently.

"Your soul will help you understand why this is happening to you at this very young age. It will help you to see how losing your friend will make you a stronger spirit in the physical world. These difficult times will strengthen your intuitive communication. Your human emotions will bond with your soul emotions. Soul emotions are those that will help you see why this is happening. The experience will force you to look at the bigger picture of how healing you can lead to healing others.

"Your internal dialogues with your guidance will provide you with answers to questions such as, 'Who Am I?' Others have disconnected from the ability to receive. It is not because they choose not to. It is because they have forgotten this open road. Stay very steady and patient when others have lost their way.

"Soon you will be sensing painful emotions among your family and friends. Everyone will be expressing his or her loss differently. It is so important that people be allowed to grieve any way they see fit. Sometimes human beings are unable to deal with the sudden death of their loved ones, and they are unable to see the bigger value of how losses will help them grow in their own spiritual life. They will cycle through continuous bouts of anger, deep sadness, confusion and resentment—the kinds of emotions you experienced in the beginning after you heard the unfortunate news.

"We do not want you to live your life in this sad state of affairs. Our job today is to instill another way of looking at these types of events: it is a way that will bring you into the circle of life rather than keep you on the outside of the circle, wanting in. I know it does not seem like you will ever get past this sad moment. However, it will make you stronger in the end because you will begin to see how all the pieces of your life fit together and create your own spiritual identity. Please hold tightly to what we have shown and told you today. Rely on your own spiritual "gut" wisdom. If something in the world is not lining up with what you sense intuitively, you have the right to question the situation. Make your own spiritual judgments. Check in with both your revered religious and profound spiritual wisdom. Forever ask yourself these soul-healing questions: "What does my soul need right now to heal? What can I do to help others soulfully heal?"

The guides left with these parting words:

"We will be with you everywhere you go from this day forth. We will not interfere with your interactions unless you ask. When invited, we will be open to any communication or questions you may have. Bless you, little one, be brave in the world with your spiritual ways and always stand true in who you are."

With this, they were gone. After their sudden departure, I was truly and finally alone with my own thoughts, feelings and memories. I knew I would soon have to leave my room and face the turmoil outside.

After the discussion, I was tired and my cup was over-flowing with TMSI (Too much spiritual information) for one session. Whether my mother was out searching for me, or I for her, we somehow crossed paths in the hallway between bedrooms. My mother and I were, and are, very close. I could immediately sense by the look on her face that she had been privy to the same devastating news about the death of my friend. She was tearing up but trying to maintain composure in an endearing, motherly attempt to avoid frightening me in any way. We gazed at one another's tear-stained faces, literally sensing the other's feelings without an exchange of words. I was bracing myself for the dreaded question: Did I know what had happened to my friend that morning?

Once she was able to gather her composure, my mother asked me just that. Hearing the question from her must have snapped me back into "real time." The hours spent with my guides now seemed like something from a timeless dream state. I had listened to every crucial insight the angels were sharing and downloaded the broadcast into the hard drive of my memory. They had somehow made the event appear so natural, in theory at least. I had listened to their explanations of what happens when a person dies and how the departed is transformed back into spirit. I had heard that communicating through soul language allows those who pass away to remain part of our lives. These explanations had seemed so reasonable and complete. It was practical, insightful wisdom presented in a way I could make sense of. All of my questions had been answered, and I had achieved a sense of peace, having already experienced the worst. Back in my room, I had supposed that the lessons I received would grant me the privilege of skipping past the pain that others would experience. Naively, I had assumed that I would be able to detach from the severe reactions others were going through.

Despite the guidance I had received, seeing my mother brought me right back to my initial state of grief. Though I cannot recall the exact conversation following our initial exchange, I know I was besieged by painful feelings again, and my mom's state of obvious distress served to unnerve me almost as much as the loss of my friend. I began to wonder what she had been doing when I was receiving the information from my guides. Had she received a similar message?

My guides had advised me to turn toward my religious practice and seek out the assistance of significant people around me. I was prepared to do this as I stood before my mother. I waited for her to do her part and to confirm what I had just experienced. I thought she might have been spending the last couple of hours with her own spiritual angels, listening to similar information. But the sharing of angelic guidance was not at all what transpired between us.

It felt as though both of us were watching repeats of the movie of my friend being hit by the car. Both of us stood there, viewing this tragic tale once again. But while the opening scenes were the same for both of us, the movies we watched veered off into two directions with very different endings. Her version left the tragic story with an abrupt ending and left out the concluding soul lessons.

My mother struggled with what to say to me. She did her best to offer comforting words and hugs, but she seemed to know that what she offered was not enough. My angels had told me that some people would not be able to process and embrace a greater understanding of death. Perhaps my own mother was one of those people. She was not saying anything that sounded remotely like what the angels had recited. She uttered the usual condolences and offered nothing that hinted at a higher understanding of the events that had occurred. A familiar, sinking feeling was rising to the surface of my being. It seemed that once again, everyone was on a different spiritual page than I was.

Regardless of the differing perspectives on death, I saw that my friend's passing deeply touched the entire tight-knit community. Over the course of several days, many well-meaning adults tried to offer me solace as they made references to heaven, God and death. But discussion of the tragedy was a painful topic, as well as socially awkward for them. What could anyone say to console a child who had lost a friend?

The adults were trying hard to offer soothing words and to help me make sense of it all. The truth was that the matter was already "all right" with me. The grown-ups, of course, did not realize that I was actually fairly well equipped, thanks to my guides, to cope with this difficult situation. There was however, one adult I wanted to speak to regarding the loss of my friend: I wanted to hear directly from my father where my friend had gone. After all, he was my religious mentor as well as my father.

The honest answer he provided was what I needed to hear. Making the most sense of all the adults who had commented, he said, "We have to *trust* that we know where she went: your friend went to heaven."

His calm demeanor and certainty were what I needed. His trust in the promise of eternal life confirmed what I had heard from my guides. What had been expressed in my bedroom was in alignment with my religion's promise of life ever after. Somehow, I had needed reassurance that I could trust both sources of knowledge.

But even my father did not mention the promises my angels had discussed with me. There was no conversation about what happens after death, no mention of the connection that remains afterward, or of the exquisite spiritual relationship that can occur between heavenly angels and awakened human beings. I knew it was possible to remain close to my childhood friend, to continue chatting as girls do. The twist was that one friend resided in the physical realm, the other in the spirit realm. But the distance could be breached, and I could live in the promise of an ongoing relationship with her and with anyone else who passed from this life to the other side, as in the spiritual union of the Communion of Saints. We have the opportunity to grow together in spirit love even after we are physically separated.

Despite this understanding, I admit that I began to second-guess myself and sunk into a bout of denial for a brief time. Maybe I had imagined the conversation with my angelic guides. Perhaps none of it had ever really happened. As I sadly watched others around me grieving, I realized that I did not want to end up like them. They tried to heal their sorrow, but the healing stopped with their minds and bodies. The healing of the soul as discussed by my guides was completely neglected. Forgetting the soul, those around me never received the full answer and instead continued to exist in a state of spiritual uncertainty.

Rather than opening the door to the promise of enlighten-ment, many left ajar the door to cynical non-believing; they kept wondering where God was in all this human suffering. Along this line of thinking, one might ask, "Why wasn't God there to save my friend?" It would also lead one to relive the tragedy over and over again. Subjected to the doubts of others, I prayed for a message that would confirm the reality of what my guides had told me in my room. Then, out of nowhere, came the mantra I had heard over and over in my bedroom: "You will forever remember every feeling, every sensation, every word we share in these moments together." The refrain sounded loud and clear as the words resonated deep within me. It was all I needed to hear to get me back on the spiritual track.

The experience of my personal loss left me with a deeper understanding of my own spiritual identity. I realized, for one, that I was able to communicate with the other side for a purpose other than mere entertainment. This ability would help me dis-cover my own unique way of serving the universe. Secondly,

I began to understand that we are all composed of a trinity of mind, body and spirit. All three elements must be in balance in order for healing to occur.

The mind thinks its way through problems.
The body reacts it way through and
the soul senses its way out of pain.

To develop spiritually, the issues or problems that arise in each of the three components must be addressed. Only when healing is accomplished on all levels can a higher consciousness be reached. Though grief over a painful situation might continue, these painful thoughts and emotions must be accepted and dealt with in order to progress along the path of enlightenment.

In order to achieve complete healing, experiences must be put into their proper spiritual perspective. This ongoing process encourages the internal seeker in all of us to expand the scope of spiritual identity, or to grow into mature souls. As we progress and grow, we move along an endless continuum that leads us closer and closer to spiritual bliss on earth.

You might ask how the experience of losing a best friend could possibly lead one closer to spiritual bliss. It happens, in fact, when the apparent tragedy is transformed into a teaching moment for those left behind. In my case, extreme anger and grief led me to ask the greatest questions that face each one of us at one time or another: "Who am I, and what is the purpose of my life?" The profound loss also led me to ask which specific spiritual lessons I needed to gain from the experience and how I could incorporate the profound wisdom I discovered into my ongoing journey toward spiritual self-awareness.

Fortunately, I was able to assimilate the lessons my guides

taught me into my daily life. I emerged from the loss with an unwavering alliance to God and to my way of communicating with the unseen world through the language of spiritual intuitive sensing. This form of communication provided my soul with answers that would otherwise have remained inaccessible. These answers were simple yet profound and were offered in a loving, non-threatening way. It has been my privilege to transcribe these conversations both for my own benefit and for the benefit of those who care to listen. Honoring God in my heart, I have embraced this innate language—it holds the ability to heal hearts and ease human conflicts.

With this realization, I understood that from this point on, there would be two paradigms working within me. I would not give up either the traditional framework of my religious upbringing or the direct spiritual knowledge accessed through intuitive sensing. Letting go of either would create a spiritual death of my own making. It would be a shameful act against the One who sent the gift in the first place.

Each of us has the ability to embrace the gift of intuitive language, or spiritual intuitive sensing. It is a gift that can be accessed at any time, once balance between body, mind and soul has been achieved. At any age, we can remain open to the divine conversation. In the next chapter, I will share simple techniques to help you embrace your own intuitive language. This language will open your soul to endless spiritual possibilities and guide you to your highest destiny.

Your innate intuitive language leads the way to the discovery of your soul-enlightened intentions—that which you were born to do.

6

SECOND SOUL LESSON

Awakening to Your
Intuitive Voice

In the first soul lesson, you evaluated the balance between heavenly and earthly energies residing within you. In each of us, the two energetic elements mix to create a unique recipe. Both components are powerful and useful in their own ways. Problems can occur, however, when one form of energy excessively dominates over the other. Favoring either the heavenly, ethereal energy or the earthly, intellectual energy can actually damage the soul and impede spiritual growth. In this second lesson, you will become more aware of your energy patterns or rhythms. When you become cognizant of the rhythms, you become more spiritually awake. You also prepare to access your natural ability to communicate with your soul—to learn the language of spiritual intuitive sensing.

Creation has been set up to allow all human beings an experience of infinite lessons. The knowledge gained from these lessons propels us forward along the road of spiritual progression. There are many religious and spiritual teaching aids at our disposal to help us along this path. These include prayer, meditation, mantras and the most misunderstood and underutilized tool of all—spiritual intuitive sensing. It is through the art of intuitive sensing that the soul derives its character and personality and develops its virtues. It is the mechanism that connects us to the realm of spirit and gives a deeper meaning to our daily lives.

There are no written instructions or guidelines on how to develop your own form of spiritual communication. It is a language that does not develop at all unless you take the initiative to learn. Throughout the ages, scholars have explored spiritual linguistics and attempted to convey abstract meanings to the world through symbols or words. The words *heaven* and *hell* are both symbols for intangible realms beyond our intellectual understanding. The ultimate satisfaction comes when you develop your own vocabulary of words, phrases and symbols to describe the connections between your conscious mind and your soul.

I now pause to caution you that we have arrived at the crossroad in the story where some may start to feel squeamish about the choices I am presenting. It is one thing to read about someone else's spiritual curiosities. It is something entirely different when you are invited to engage in the same experience. In this case, I am asking you to reinstate your own intuitive sensing capabilities. This is the point where the waters get murky in the religious pool of thought. You might feel as though you are being pushed right up against core religious boundaries.

How do you decide what is an honest and natural practice leading to spiritual awakening and what is a harmful and artificial practice? How far can you travel down the path of the mystical unknown before crossing the line into perceived "heresy" or evil action? Most of us want to believe we are in a state of grace with our heavenly master. I certainly do. In all honestly, I can say without hesitation that my interactions and conversations with the other side have never led me to engage in behavior that has challenged my fundamental religious teachings. It is my belief that the intuitive interactions I experienced after my childhood friend's death all those years ago served to deepen the bond between my soul and God. I believe the strength of this bond casts out any evil force that would dare to cross it. That being said, I am not asking you to replicate my personal experiences, nor do I suggest that this is possible. However, I do offer the possibility that intuition can play a significant role in the accomplishment of your own spiritual life goals.

I would venture to guess that some of you might already be utilizing the language of spiritual intuitive sensing. Others might have forgotten this tool but are ready to reclaim it. Either way, the effort of developing your skills in intuitive language is well worth the effort.

Spiritual Intuitive Sensing: Higher Religious Education

The diagram below demonstrates the spiritual intuitive sensing blueprint that you energetically inherit at birth.

Original Soul Intuitive Blueprint: Spiritual Innocence

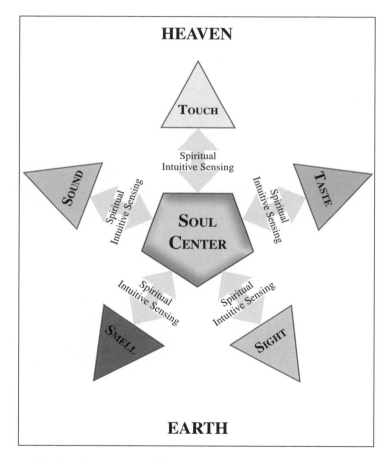

Notice the center of the star. As within your physical being, the soul resides in the center. In some schools of thought, this area is referred to as the "inner child." All divine insights initiate from this pure, innocent center and resonate outward. It is your connection to the heavenly realm. When you examine the diagram, you can see that intuition is connected to the five senses. Others have theorized that intuition is the "sixth sense." In my view, intuitive sensing is not a separate sense. Rather, it is a basic property that resides within you and manifests through the other senses.

Your intuition is constantly in communication with you through your five senses. Through sight, sound, touch, taste and smell, intuitively sent messages are received via an intricate network of electrical pathways. Your senses translate these messages so that they can be expressed in the physical world. Your senses are a means of broadcasting your "soul voice" and communicating with other souls. They are the means of transforming transparent images and impressions from other realities into human experience.

Unlike an "inner child," which is fixed in time, your spiritual soul grows and expands as you do. It is a constant work in progress. As the soul evolves, however, it does not have to work through any "issues," as a child often does. The soul is always sheltered and protected from outside drama—it is like a miniature reflection of the supreme light itself. While we must sometimes force our bodies and minds to address our life challenges, the soul is self-motivated at all times to work through its spiritual lessons.

Reclaiming your spiritual innocence requires that you get in touch with your own spiritual intuitive sensing. This intuitive language consists of symbols that are imprinted on your unconscious mind as well as visions, sounds, and tastes and conscious "self-talk." The elements of the language evolve and grow over time and are congruent with your stage in life. In other words, the vocabulary and symbolic cues you assimilated at the age of three are not the same as what you have assimilated at the age of forty.

To awaken and to begin to access your spiritual intuitive language takes time and practice. Your soul is always striving to communicate its spiritual insights and pushing you to discover elusive mystical wisdom. The process prompts all of us to stay alert and to focus on our highest purpose for existence.

I can certainly understand the hesitation many of you have toward reclaiming this kind of interactive spirituality. After all, many of us have seen examples of people who have taken the gift of intuition to the extreme. There is a fine line between manipulation and respectful understanding of this unassuming energetic force. Those who are not equipped to handle the gift properly can get caught up in what I call the "Hollywood stage" of awakening; they are more concerned with using their intuitive wisdom to assume control over situations or other people than in understanding God's calling. When you commit yourself to an authentic spiritual life, however, there is very little room for the flaunting of ego. The rewards of joy, abundance and tranquility become much more fulfilling than dominance over others.

EBB AND FLOW OF SPIRITUAL INTUITIVE SENSING

As we have already established, two energies, heavenly and earthly, influence your spiritual personality. At various phases in your life, one or the other type of energy might dominate. Discovering your divine energy rhythm is the first step to connecting with your spiritual intuitive language.

Each type of energy is associated with the specific type of life lesson you are learning at the moment. Heavenly energy is aligned with the "art of being," which is concerned with spiritual lessons. Earthly energy is aligned with the "art of doing," which is concerned with physical lessons.

In order to adapt and thrive in each phase, it is helpful to recognize which phase you are currently experiencing. By doing so, you will move from the path of passive observer to the path of interactive spiritual participant. This is a joyful experience, akin to being in an awakened meditative state.

To a certain extent, both heavenly and earthly energies are always moving through us. However, more times than not, a prominent energy phase will appear. The following exercise is designed to help you understand your own energy patterns, or divine rhythm. You will learn to see how these energy patterns lead you to certain behaviors in the world and how your actions in the world are a reflection of your dominant energy force.

CHARTING YOUR DIVINE ENERGY RHYTHM

To identify your energy rhythm, you will need to figure out which type of energy is driving your actions over a period of time. It means literally examining how many minutes, hours or days you stay in any one phase. Through this accounting, you will learn how much or how little you are connected with both heavenly and earthly intuitive cues from the universe.

It is best to complete this exercise over a period of two weeks, though a month is actually preferable. It can take this long for an identifiable pattern to emerge.

EXERCISE ONE: THE ART OF DOING VERSUS THE ART OF BEING

STEP 1   On day one, read the description of each energy phase (the Art of Doing and the Art of Being) as written below. Read them aloud when you are alone in a quiet room. Do not draw any conclusions from this information or form any expectations about what you might discover. Just let the information marinate in your brain and soul on the first day.

THE ART OF DOING

In this phase, you undertake tasks that require energy associated with the earth. These are often tasks in which considerable physical activity is required. In general, this phase is concerned with working and achieving goals. Many people enjoy the stage of *doing*. When you are in this phase, it may appear to the outside world that you are productive and successful. Even the religious world tends to look favorably upon those who are actively participating in the art of doing.

In this stage, you have an opportunity to see how your actions in the physical world are reflections of the spiritual messages you receive during the art of being.

ACTIVITIES ASSOCIATED WITH THE ART OF DOING

Exercise, career-related tasks, engaging in "bottom heavy" thinking, spontaneous activities, courageous and heroic acts, intense or complex intellectual efforts.

THE ART OF BEING

This phase is associated with moments of prayer, reflection and quiet seclusion from the outside world. It exists in environments that capture the essence of heavenly energy. Unlike the art of doing—which requires physical action—this phase demands that you focus attention on the soul. It is a time when others might label your actions as unproductive or lazy, as the inner activity often goes unnoticed.

For example, when I was with the angels in my bedroom, I was not physically doing anything—I was just listening to the messages from the other side. There was nothing for me to do but remain present in mind and soul. I was being tutored in how to embrace the art of being and how to be a good listener and receiver.

The lessons of this phase are associated with finding the deeper significance of events happening in your exterior life. It is the stage where you consider the reasons why events have occurred.

Those who are accustomed to a busy life of action are less likely to enjoy the "art of being." Many are disinclined to sit around and wait for intuitive messages. However, this phase is not about doing *nothing*. It is about stepping out of the daily chaos, recharging the soul and waiting for the right time to move back into the phase of *doing*. It is a time to regroup and consider the next life lessons to be undertaken. Without these spiritual timeouts, you cannot learn how God's wisdom is conveyed through the subtle voice of the soul. Moreover, you find yourself repeating the same spiritual lessons over and over again.

ACTIVITIES AND THOUGHTS ASSOCIATED WITH THE ART OF BEING

Contemplation, introspection, prayer, silence, "top heavy" thinking, faith, free-flowing ideas, simplicity, reflection, meditation, heightened sense of awareness,

STEP 2   On day two, you will need a notebook. You can label it "Spiritual Intuitive Handbook." On this day you will allow the universe to give you cues about which energy phase you are experiencing. Do not make an effort to pay attention. Just become aware of whatever seeps through to your conscious mind. As they arise throughout the day, record any identifiable words, symbols, actions or conscious thoughts that seem to stand out or come to you. Record the entries in a list format, making additions as often as you like. Record whenever you feel inspired to do so. You might want to doodle in the book or add a drawing or two.

I know this sounds tedious, but there is a method here. I still carry sticky notes with me at all times in order to catch information that comes to me throughout the day. At the end of the day, I add the message(s) to my intuitive notebook.

Your notebook will become an essential tool, which you will refer to later, in Soul Lesson Three. Continue to make entries in your notebook until a routine has been established and the intuitive language you are recording becomes familiar to you. After a certain point in time, writing in your book will become second nature. At this point, you can document only when you feel a particular need to do so.

STEP 3   Periodically, you need to label each individual entry in your notebook as belonging to either the "art of being" or the "art of doing" phase. You may refer to the examples above when considering how to categorize the entries, but you may find that you have an intuitive sense of where each word or phrase fits. This is a creative and subjective process where you are encouraged to use your imagination!

STEP 4 Continue this process every day for at least two weeks. Near day four you will begin to see patterns among the intuitive words that have floated to the surface of your conscious mind. As you continue to write in your notebook, your divine energy rhythm will present itself from the apparent randomness of your entries.

Your next task is to identify this pattern. There should be movements from the phase of being to the phase of doing, and from the phase of doing to the phase of being. The words and phrases associated with each phase you have identified are part of your spiritual vocabulary—your language of spiritual intuitive sensing. There is a purpose to this language: it offers clues to your life lessons, decisions and challenges.

By mapping your intuitive language system over your divine energy rhythm, you will start to make intellectual sense of the messages from both the physical world and the heavenly realm. In this way, the natural communication style of the soul will be restored to its original, intuitive blueprint.

Perhaps you were seeking a more direct interpretation of the entries you recorded in your intuitive notebook. Many hope to discover the grand *Aha* moment to validate this type of intuitive awareness. Feeling disappointed when the moment never arrives, they completely miss the mystic relevance of what they have discovered. The true *Aha* moment comes with the realization there is a natural simplicity to the soul's voice and that each and every waking moment is filled with mystery and wonder. Spiritual intuitive language will only work for you if you are willing to commit to the slow and steady expansion of your mind, body, and spirit.

THE EFFECTS OF ROTE LEARNING ON SPIRITUAL INTUITIVE SENSING

When you learn information by rote, it is easy to lose your connection to your soul and spiritual intuitive sensing. Rote learning involves quick memorization without deep understanding. It is like cramming for a test and achieving nothing but a recall of facts. This type of learning has become a common habit for many of us. In regard to religion, rote learning allows us to learn the catechism rather than question the content of the material. It sometimes keeps us from upsetting the proverbial applecart.

Living by rote has become a way of life for many of us. We eat the same foods every day; we go to the same gym year after year—same time each day. There is a certain comfort in these daily routines. But if we always insist on adhering to what is predictable, we do not allow ourselves the opportunity to experience the spontaneity of spirit in our lives.

At church I have witnessed the negative impact of living by rote. Intent on being "church-going" and adhering to every religious protocol, it is possible to become a "spiritual casualty" and lose the excitement of living in the moment. Spiritual intuitive sensing is a way of awakening to the possibility each day offers. Though you might fear that engaging in spiritual intuitive sensing is crossing over into forbidden territory, this type of communication is nothing but your soul throwing you hints, if only you will listen. The soul is vying for your attention, enticing you to join the world of spontaneous reality, to energize your sleepy routine and grasp the grand possibilities of the mystery of your life.

EXERCISE 2: BREAKING ROTE HABITS

The easiest way to avoid falling into rote spiritual habits is to maintain a constant mode of internal questioning. But rather than asking themselves questions, many make the mistake of turning to outside sources—often consulting other humans or angel guides—for information. Others might seek out new circumstances or a new environment in an attempt to find answers to life's questions. I suggest that you do the opposite: you need to ask yourself the right questions before you make a decision or take action. Your soul voice is always in conversation with your intellect. It will always be considering what the next lesson or step ought to be.

When communicating with your soul, pose a simple but universal question first: Ask: "What is the next step for me?" In the beginning, do not wait in anticipation for the answer. Let your intuitive language do its internal magic. When the time is right, the answer will present itself. Slowly, after time, begin asking more specific questions. For instance, you might ask: "What lessons have I learned from the experience?"

REMAIN ALERT FOR SUBTLE MESSAGES

On occasion I have wondered how my spiritual life would have developed if I had chosen to ignore the angelic guidance I was given on the tragic day my friend was killed. I might have succumbed to my fears and insecurities, fled my bedroom and missed the opportunity. Somehow, in the midst of the turmoil that day, I allowed myself to ask the questions that led me to the spiritual lessons I received.

Your first step to receiving guidance is to identify your questions. The next step is to watch for the subtle messages or cues of your spiritual intuitive communication. Easier said than done. Most people have no patience to wait for these quiet answers. Instead, they choose to push forward in spite of their confusion, or they simply ignore the subtle messages they graciously received. This kind of impatience will not lead to the goal of communicating through spiritual intuitive sensing.

EXERCISE 3: LEARNING TO PAY ATTENTION AND FOCUS

It is futile to attempt to reinstate your connection with intuitive language unless you are a good listener. I was able to develop my spiritual communication at a young age because I learned to listen to the voice within. One of the greatest benefits of intuitive sensing is the ability to focus on matters of high priority. It helps you to eliminate all the distractions and focus on the straight and narrow path leading to the most essential, spiritually-oriented goals. As you learn to listen to your soul voice, external distractions will exert less control over your internal thoughts and listening will become easier.

I love the power of meditative phrases or mantras; reciting the right phrase is an effective tool for focusing your attention. You can use the following phrase when you find your thoughts are wandering: *I am in full command of my attention and choose to focus on the moment at hand.*

You can use this mantra or create your own to bring your attention to the present moment and quiet yourself enough to listen. The incredible gift of soul communication requires that you remain constantly receptive. Every message is presented in new and creative ways. While the spiritual meaning or lesson might remain the same, the message is never presented the same way twice; it changes in order to capture your attention.

Commit to listening and paying attention to your soul voice in short increments of time. Many set themselves up for failure because they attempt to change their lives and master the lesson all at once. This approach will not work in this case, because intuitive language is sporadic. Sometimes the soul voice sends continuous messages, while other times it allows us to find our own answers within our external explorations. The key is to know when to pay attention, listen and focus.

LASTLY, TAKE RESPONSIBILITY: LIVE IT AS YOU LEARNED IT

Many people gravitate toward using spiritual intuitive language in order to avoid mistakes or painful consequences in life. If you find yourself in this category, please rethink your motives. It is true that the tools of intuitive sensing can help guide you through any number of spiritual, practical or religious lessons. However, an attempt to use this gift to avoid making the wrong decision will not work to your advantage. Intuitive sensing encourages one to celebrate every choice. It does not give us the "right" answer, but rather allows us the opportunity to make "mistakes" without judgments and to grow from our experiences.

The soul itself does not have preconceived labels of right and wrong. It exists in a place without judgments and is only concerned with learning. When the soul communicates with us, it is our responsibility to respond with respect and gratitude for the higher source from which all insights and wisdom originate.

Finally, remember that spiritual intuitive language is

meant to complement decisions based upon informed thought and input derived from the five senses. It is not meant to replace rational thinking. It is a gift from God and must be used with the greatest care and respect.

The human soul loves new adventures. It is a thrill-seeker, disinterested in living a safe routine. Charting its own course of action, the soul is interested in what lies ahead, what lessons are yet to be learned. It requires time and dedication to become aware of the soul's wants and needs.

When you choose to live a soul-based life, it's as though your clock is reset to a different time zone. Our souls do not acknowledge time limitations. However long it takes one to learn spiritual lessons is however long it takes. There is no race to the finish line. While the human side of us gets caught up in "doing" and "accomplishing," our souls are more interested in "being" and "learning."

Learning to live an awakened, spiritual life takes patience and practice, especially if these concepts are new to you. Grant yourself permission to take as long as it takes to develop your unique way of communicating with your soul. Work at your own pace, knowing that this process offers you new hope and can lead the way to a better future. At the very least, listening to the subtle calling of your soul will lead to a deeper awareness of God's constant presence in your life.

7

The Church In the City

You have to move when the Spirit moves you. That was literally true in the case of my family. My stay in the spiritual Eden of our Missouri hillside church drew to a close as my father announced his call to a new church in the big city. I was a preteen and reluctant to leave, but my father promised adventures awaiting us in our new church home. The next few years would prove to be a time of losing my way in the much larger and more diverse metropolitan congregation.

The first thing that struck me when we arrived in the city was the noise. Coming from the countryside, everything seemed so loud by comparison. My senses were in overdrive. From sunup to sundown, there was no place to escape the cacophony of sounds in the streets. The sweet country air was replaced with the scent of exhaust fumes. The spacious yards and green trees were replaced with row upon row of tract housing.

Upon arrival I was immediately homesick. While I missed my friends terribly, what I really pined for was something less tangible. My longing came from deep inside my soul; I was missing the silence, the peaceful scenery outside my back door, the ethereal colors radiating from the trees and the angels hidden among the bushes.

For the first time, I was separated from my angelic friends. Without their familiar presence, I felt very much alone and exposed in my new city environment. I found it hard to believe that our time together was over. After years of conversation, I had become accustomed to their insights and guidance from the other side. We had been walking this spiritual journey in tandem, or so I thought.

All I could think about was how difficult it would be for the angels to find me amidst the crowded maze of steel and concrete. The move was both physically and emotionally unsettling. Everything in this urban environment seemed larger than life from my middle-school perspective—bigger houses, wider roads and even a grander church.

If all this were not enough of a culture shock, there also were many new faces to meet and greet. Back in small-town Missouri, I had felt comfortable with our small congregation of a few dozen. In this new church, there were not dozens of members—there were hundreds. I felt lost, a country girl in this diverse, energetic metropolitan parish.

But at least I was familiar with the routine of starting out at a new church. Just as when we arrived at the hillside church, the community of the city church was excited by the arrival of a new minister. Polite members dropped by the parsonage to welcome us with hot meals. This was my favorite part of the transition! Even though I was still not convinced that we should have moved, I was somewhat consoled that the casseroles were similar to those made by members of our old church. Perhaps this meant that the church I left behind and my new one shared some other similarities. Such was my thinking at the age of twelve.

In the hope of keeping the spiritual traditions I held dear, I wanted to investigate what other similarities there were between the two churches. In particular, I wondered if I would find my angels inside this new place of worship. I decided that I'd have to walk inside the sanctuary alone to find out. If I could sense the angelic energy, then I would know that I belonged at this church and that we were once again united.

At the first opportunity, I went off alone to enter the empty church. The sanctuary had several entrances; I chose the main door and took a deep breath. The minute I opened the door, a gust of energy rushed out with a whoosh, throwing me back a step or two. This force was completely different from what I had experienced inside my little country church, where the vibrations had been gentle and inviting, like waves rolling into shore from a calm sea. The hypnotic flow of that energy had been tender and soothing.

The vibration inside this new city church was amplified; while it was not completely different in quality from the energy I had experienced inside the country church, it was more intense. As the force hit me like bursts of warm air, I began to notice illuminated images dancing from left to right. Sometimes they ascended to the high ceiling and disappeared.

It was the confirmation I was looking for. Now I could rest comfortably with the knowledge that I was once again united with the angels. My acclimation to city life progressed more easily after this. In my bedroom I could retreat to my own quiet, personal sanctuary, just like I'd had in the country. Here I could dream and speak to my guides in peace. As I was old enough by now to be left alone, I could also enjoy time in the house when I was the only one at home.

On one occasion when everyone had left the house but me, there was a knock at the front door. In those days, it was considered safe for a young girl to answer the door when she was home alone. Without hesitation, I opened the door to find two older, well-dressed men. Each held at his side what appeared to be a tattered old Bible. I had never experienced anything like this and had no idea what the nature of their visit might be.

"Have you found Jesus?" one of the men asked me and I stared at him in confusion.

"If so, what date were you saved?" the other one asked and my expression turned to horror.

Although I'd been a practicing Christian since the day I was born, I did not know how to answer the men. I hadn't the slightest clue what they were talking about. A feeling of shame rose up within me as I continued to stare at them blankly. No one had ever told me the date I had been brought to the saving grace of Jesus Christ and had adopted Christian living. As far as I knew, I had always lived this way. According to my Sunday school teachers, I was a member of God's community through baptism. But I knew very little about religion outside my sheltered church upbringing. These men were speaking about something I had never heard before.

When I closed the door after accepting the pamphlet they handed me, I felt shaken. They had talked about Jesus "saving me." Save me from what? I wondered. Had I done something in the past to offend God? I was following all religious instructions from my church and spiritual guidance from the angels. Disappointment began to settle in. Had I not prayed enough? Had I inadvertently disobeyed the angels? I had worked hard every day to be in alignment with what was expected both religiously and spiritually. My mind jumped from question to question before I finally decided what to do next.

I was a scared twelve-year-old girl and I closed the blinds and locked the doors. I had no idea if the men would come back or if other visitors would be coming. The more I replayed the conversation in my mind, the sadder I became. I could think of nothing else until my parents returned home later that day and the story spilled out of me. Upon hearing of the visit from the two proselytizers, my father decided to hold a family meeting. He stood before us and spoke in his preacher's voice about the need for tolerance and compassion for those who followed different faith traditions. While his explanation made sense, the visit had triggered something within me; it was as though the experience had opened the gate to a religious wilderness. In this new frontier, unknown forces and man-made complexities about religious ideology threatened the simple faith of my childhood.

Shortly after the visit from the two men, I felt compelled to follow the tenets of my religious faith all the more closely. I could not completely shake the words of the visitors who had told me that I needed to be saved. The men hadn't told me exactly how to go about being "saved," so the answer was up to my own interpretation. I decided I should follow the rules of the Bible to a tee and live exactly as God intended. That also included eliminating any behavior the sacred text forbade. Once I had made this decision, I set off to be the best Christian follower ever! Of course, this was easier said than done.

At first I was able to succeed in my goal. I read the scriptures and followed the crowd. In church, it was a simple matter to pray on cue, sing in unison and stand during the important parts of the worship service. The structured format was reassuring and gave me a sense of what was expected of me as a good Christian. There were no questions to ask myself, and there were no more ethereal conversations with the other side. It was a matter of living in the moment and doing what the religious authorities told me to do next.

I enjoyed participating in my new church, and I especially enjoyed meeting many of the people who attended. I felt in fellowship with many beautiful people who had good intentions similar to mine. I felt that the majority of the parishioners were attending for the right reasons, rather than for the purpose of simply being seen at church. I truly wanted to be accepted by this kind and loving church family. I also wanted to be free to be "myself" with my church family, but I was becoming aware that I was expected to maintain a certain façade, the one required of all preachers' kids.

In order to fulfill my role and meet expectations, I was completely resolved to do whatever it took. Now a teenager,

I determined that my gift of communicating with the angels from the other side would make me an outsider. I decided this activity had been child's play anyway—it was something I did when I was younger to pass the long hours at church. I did not need the angelic help or advice anymore. I could find my own answers within the religious text in front of me. Although it was with sadness and a certain amount of remorse, I decided to close that chapter of my life for good. Not because I necessarily wanted to do so, but because "fitting in" had become all-important. I was not willing to take the risk of behaving in ways considered unorthodox by others. In retrospect, it is fairly obvious that there may have been another reason I abandoned my intuitive gift during that time: I did not want the ability to sense and intuitively know people. I loved our church family and did not want the burden of receiving so much information about people as I had in the past. It would have been more than a teenage girl could process.

At this point I had grown weary of maintaining the balancing act between my spiritual intuitive awareness and my religious practices. I was ready to serve and give myself up completely to the religious life before me. I was old enough to be in charge and decide whether or not my guides could intervene. Surely my human will was stronger than the angels' gentle invitations? The mission before me seemed straightforward. I had to control my thoughts and feelings in order to avoid any communications with the other side. In this distorted state of mind, I sincerely believed that I had, up to now, been suffering from some sort of spiritual disease; I thought it was my responsibility to cure myself of this hindrance.

There were countless days when I would get down on my knees in my bedroom and plead with my guides to go away. *Leave me alone,* I implored them. I had lost the inner strength and fortitude it took to maintain this dual existence anymore. In fact, I did my best to convince the angels and my spiritual parents that I would be fine without their guidance. *Take your spiritual intuitive language home with you to heaven*, I said. *Or give the gift to someone else who truly wants it.*

It seemed as though I had succeeded in my attempts to separate from the heavenly guides. As time went by, I could sense that the energy of the spirit world was receding into the distance. It was becoming less pronounced, though I knew it would still be there in the event of an "emergency." In truth the energy never disappeared; I just refused to listen, pay attention or act upon the messages the way I had in the past. By allowing my human ego to lead, I told myself, "I can do this all by myself!" All along, my guides knew that I would eventually come running back to my spiritual home base and soul-centered living.

At the time, I was going through typical teenage angst like every other kid I knew. Fitting in with the other kids mattered more than anything. As a minister's daughter, my entire social life revolved around church activities. My parents expected me to participate in each and every event offered to teens. As a result, all my relationships were formed through church activities, and the world beyond the church environment was little known to me. While many children grow up experiencing a variety of cultures and lifestyles, my childhood was, to a large extent, insular. I do not think this was the intention of my parents, but it was a byproduct of their dedication to the church. It was our way to sleep, eat and pray church—though not necessarily religion. Later I came to understand that those are two separate categories.

As ambassadors of the church, it was our family's responsibility to model the behavior that all other Christian families should aspire to. I was told what to say and what *not* to say in public. I was told which discussions were appropriate and which were not. In this way every church function became a staged event, down to the detail of what I was allowed to wear.

My parents could count on me to perform every time. Though I might not have felt like participating in every church social, I was on high alert to maintain outward appearances and to remain discreet about parish secrets. Living in the parsonage, I could not help but be privy to the hundreds of private stories, all shared in confidence with my father. I was also aware of the church politics, even though they were conducted behind closed doors. Then there were the inflated egos that, despite our religious upbringing, clashed over money issues. I had a difficult time understanding how these arguments reflected religious ideals. Nevertheless, we put on happy faces on Sunday morning and remained in service to others.

The assignment gave me a sense of self-importance for a brief time. Like the church elite, I bought into the idea that my role was of particular significance. I mimicked the idea that those who were not in my Christian club were somehow lacking. However, this illusion began to weaken over time and a sense of fear began to creep into my daily experience of God. It did not help that my intuitive connection to heaven was waning. I sensed that the veil separating heaven from earth was beginning to close, just as it had with the other children I had known growing up. My spiritual innocence was disappearing. At the same time, I was facing challenges that required the help of my guides. Now these problems were becoming too big for me to handle on my own.

Behind the scenes, the constant pressure was beginning to wear upon my family. It was difficult enough for my parents to raise my brother and me while caring for a small group of worshipers. When the flock tripled, so did their responsibilities and problems. Human egos butting against each other for power and control were a source of frequent discord. Religion, I learned, was a business. Those who did not toe the religious line were soon banished—not physically banished but rather shunned socially from the community. Those on the inside feared being associated with those who were not on the *right side* of the faith.

The more I assimilated into the ways of the church, the more I feared for my own position. At the same time, I began to think that this church hierarchy did not necessarily promote the purest expression of faith. Excluding others was certainly not one of the lessons I had been taught by my angels. My guides had espoused an all-inclusive spirit club where all were welcome and no one was turned away. Disheartened by the state of affairs, I began to yearn for my angelic friends once again. I wanted my old spiritual life back.

However, I was not at all sure that my guides would return to me. Perhaps, after taking this detour, I would not be allowed to experience my untainted connection to the spirit world once again. After all, they might not forgive me for turning my back on them. I could only hope they would still communicate with me, because the truth of the matter was that I needed my angels more than ever. I hoped for a sign, a symbol, or any message to let me know I would be allowed back to the spiritual home where I belonged.

Several weeks later, after silently declaring my desire to resume my intuitive life, I received the sign I had been waiting for. It was presented to me in a way I could not possibly miss.

The angels' message was revealed to me through my father. On several occasions in the past, I had seen angels come to his aid unbeknownst to him. They had always been present at church and on Sundays I had enjoyed the surprise of finding out which particular angels would be in attendance along with the humans. On the day the angels' message was revealed to me, there was a change in the usual game plan at church—a change initiated by my father.

Preaching to an audience was my father's forte. On this particular Sunday, it was the method of presentation rather than the content that was unique. Though I cannot recall what my father talked about that morning, the sermon was instrumental in bringing about my spiritual reawakening. I hope it served to awaken others who attended that day as well.

In the 1970s, cordless microphone systems were being installed in various speaking arenas, including both large and small sanctuaries. This technological advance changed the way a speaker could communicate; a cumbersome microphone cord was no longer needed and this allowed the speaker to move freely about the stage. After our church was blessed with one of these new sound systems, my father thought to test out the equipment in an unconventional way: he decided to give his weekly sermon from his office instead of from the pulpit.

So it was that although we were seated in the pews, we could hear but not see him. My first reaction was pure delight. For the first time in my life, it seemed that others were experiencing the word of God in the way that I had experienced my guides. There was no physical presence, just a voice commanding attention. Those in attendance were forced to stop looking at the messenger for cues and were forced instead to search inside themselves for answers. The pulpit where "he" was supposed to be was empty. It was as though his voice was coming directly from Heaven itself!

I surveyed the church as my father began to recite his rehearsed script. It was buzzing with the audience's strong reactions. My intuitive sensing moved into action and picked up all the colors, sounds, and sights being emitted with the emotional fireworks.

I then noticed that the area around the altar was crowded with dozens of laughing angels; they were rejoicing in the unconventionality of it all. Their hands were in the air as though to calm those in the crowd who were nervous. Light was bouncing off the walls and ceiling like a laser show. Happily, I took in these sights—unmistakable signs from the angels. Once again, I was being welcomed back into the world of spiritual intuitive sensing. After settling down, my attention returned to the crowd.

You could cut the human panic with a knife. No one knew what to do next. Their weekly religious ritual had been taken away from them without their consent. How dare my father present the scriptures of the day without proper protocol! They had two alternatives: get up and leave or accept the new spiritual lesson. They were being invited to learn about the process of hearing the unseen. They could choose to be discontented observers or interactive spiritual participants. The choice was now theirs.

The reactions were priceless. At first, everyone continued to gaze at the place my father ought, by custom, to have been—the pulpit. Once they realized he was not going to appear, they began to focus on others around them. They gauged how their neighbors were reacting to the experience. I could sense the mind-set: the congregation was split right down the middle. Half were embracing the religious challenge whereas the other half felt as though they were in purgatory and had been betrayed or cheated. Everyone had come expecting the usual ritualistic show—the pomp and circumstance they expected to be on display every week at the same time and in the same place.

Those who felt punished were shutting down immediately. They had no desire whatsoever to accept a message from a minister hiding behind the walls. It would apparently take a stunt even bigger than this to rock their spiritual intuitive sensing into action!

The quiet listeners approached the sermon differently. Like me, many of these Christians accepted the lesson with open arms. It didn't matter that the messenger could not be seen; what mattered were the words being imparted. Those of us who listened grew together in our spiritual intuitive sensing that day.

I was gradually finding my way back after having lost it in the new city church. In little more than a year, I had gone from one extreme to the other. Viewing my ability to receive angelic messages as some sort of impediment, I had tried to abandon this part of myself. But there was a point when I found I did not particularly care for the person I was becoming. Try as I might to turn my back on my intuitive sensing, subtle voices found their way back into my consciousness.

The experience of losing, then finding, my guides left me with a greater appreciation and understanding of the intuitive gifts I had received. Finally, I understood that they had been with me in the trenches all along. Though I had turned my back on them, they had been sending me subtle hints, trying to help me find my way back to my spiritual home. In the same way, your guides are sending you hints, vying for your attention and hoping to assist you as you journey closer to God.

8

Living the Process of God

When I was growing up in our countryside church, I was dedicated to keeping the channels of intuitive communication open. At that time, messages from my guides as well as cues from Mother Earth offered an array of lessons and these arrived unfiltered by humans. When I became a teenager, this connection was tested to the limits. At our new church in the city, the lessons I assimilated came directly from people and from the refined, polished practice of organized religion.

The spiritual awareness I eventually developed was still in cocoon form during my teen and early adult years. For a long while, I remained tucked away under my father's protective cloak of religion. Sheltered in this way, I felt safe because no one questioned my religious dedication. At this stage in my spiritual evolution, I was still gathering information and formulating ideas. I didn't have the words to articulate what I was experiencing internally or to express my beliefs. In my mid-to-late twenties, I began to appreciate the duality of my spiritual and religious experiences.

I relished my spiritual anonymity,
Remained reclusive with the untainted spirit world
until I was ready for rebirth from my religious cocoon
into an active awakened etheric butterfly.

My particular sect of Christianity is considered mainstream by most. The faith allowed some room for a degree of individual interpretation and expression. Though I was never told that the use of my intuitive gifts was explicitly forbidden, for a time, I avoided the conscious use of my talents, especially when it came to interpreting the behavior of others. Although I did not make an effort to develop these skills, nonetheless my intuitive language was growing exponentially. The fact that I was in constant contact with my father's parishioners certainly had an effect upon my gift; the exposure to so many emotional and physical states helped me develop awareness of the human condition and hone my intuitive abilities.

Growing up as a minister's daughter, I developed an appreciation for the lessons learned from the happiness and heartbreaks of others. While a teacher or parent can teach some life lessons, other truths can only be conveyed when another reflects back to you what you need to see or hear. Learning from these types of experiences was a valuable gift given to me by the church. At my father's parish, I witnessed the power of God's love bringing together total strangers. When you watch others being moved by the experience of prayer and worship, this can give you the confidence to know that you also have the capacity to love and be loved by both God and others, unconditionally.

I saw love being shared between all types of "soul mates"—between parents and children, children and their friends or siblings, minister and church members, members and their friends or significant others. Most impressive of all was the love humans expressed for the mystery of God. It was life-changing to witness people conquering difficult challenges because their souls were touched by divine love. People from all walks of life, many of whom endured an array of devastating circumstances, believed in miracles and allowed God's healing work to be done. The church offered their souls a place to rest and to release their burdens. As part of a congregation sharing in the hardships and hopes of others, you acquire empathy for others.

Despite the lessons I was learning at the church, there came a point when I began to lose my way spiritually. I was no longer making core decisions about my relationship with God from within. Somehow along the line, this responsibility had been turned over to others—to people who thought they knew what was best for my highest good. As a teenager, I felt a growing resentment toward some adults at church. Most of them displayed outward signs of piety and spoke appropriately, yet I could sense discord between their words and actions. Their behavior in the world was not reflecting their professed convictions. Gradually, I began to realize that some of the adults in the congregation were leading double lives.

Although I recognized their hypocrisy, it was my responsibility to treat each person who attended the church services with love and with as much respect as humanly possible. I was following that command to the best of my ability. However, it did not seem fair to me that I was expected to follow the rules and others were not. These individuals arrived at church outwardly portraying themselves in ways diametrically opposed to their inner personas. These charades utterly missed the whole point of the spiritual exercise of going to church to find grace and forgiveness.

As I continued to observe others, I began to receive hints that I should return to the game I played in church as a child and seek intuitive guidance. My childhood ability to sense the color hues surrounding all living creatures had become more pronounced over time. Without even realizing it, I often accessed this form of intuitive language. When I observed the colors around certain individuals at church, I noticed that their colors were neither the usual shades of the rainbow nor were they black—they were gray.

I fully grasp the concept of church as a place of welcome for all troubled souls. The church offers guidance to those in spiritual need. The love, prayers and lessons presented each week are supposed to bring about change and healing. For some people at our church, however, the transition never occurred. It was as if their gray hues were acting as shields preventing them from accessing their soul centers. They preferred to stay stuck, going through a meaningless routine of religious observation, rather than fire up the spark of spiritual awakening. They had given up all hopes of ever finding soul innocence once again. This condition worried me. Was this my future if I remained in this environment?

Something else began to bother me as well. During my childhood, my spiritual path had wandered wherever my soul decided to take me. I was open to the lessons as they appeared and as I needed them. But in church, the Sunday school lessons were always preplanned for us, regardless of whether or not the lessons pertained to our particular needs or concerns at the time. As a child, I had been able to supplement the Sunday school curriculum with the instruction provided by my guides. When I became a teenager and stopped listening to the messages from the other side and focused solely on the lessons taught at church, I lost my spiritual alignment. My new commitment to the standard religious curriculum was narrowing the focus of my expression of creativity, of my imagination and my sensitivity to intuitive clues. I was inadvertently becoming like the Sunday school teachers.

Though I tried hard for a time to ignore my intuitive knowledge, it began to haunt me and lead me to question organized religion in general. The pressure was slowly rising inside. As a teenage girl, my need to stay emotionally and socially connected to people in my community was greater than my need to explore my spirituality. As a result, I sacrificed pieces of myself in order to fit in. When I stopped communicating with my soul, I stopped asking difficult questions, such as, "Why can't I be friends with those people?" Or, "Why should I treat the ones over there differently?" I was becoming too bottom heavy with intellectual religious dogma and losing touch with my top heavy intuitive sensing. When the questions finally arose, I began to verbalize them aloud. The answers I received from my parents were often, "Because I said so."

Within the religious wilderness that was my church environment, I discovered that one's spirit journey often takes a more winding course than one's traditional faith journey. The traditional religious journey is usually a planned, predetermined path from beginning to end. The spirit journey, however, meanders and creates its own course. The unpredictability of the spirit journey is what feeds into the fears of many uninformed religious followers and leads them to reject a more personal exploration of their spirituality. It seems easier and safer when you are told what to believe rather than venturing into the world of the unknown and developing your own interior life.

After hearing these apparent criticisms, you might arrive at the conclusion that I have a love-hate relationship with my Christianity. This could not be further from the truth, for even the difficulties I faced at church taught me valuable spiritual lessons. For instance, I consider the two Bible-carrying men who came to my front door years ago to be "physical angels."

Physical angels are those who show up in your life out of nowhere. They cross your path at a point in time and empower you with insights—both practical and spiritual—that exceed your ability to comprehend at the moment. They may offer a series of life lessons, learning that comes compacted into a flicker of time. Even though they may exit your life as quickly as they arrive, they leave an imprint on your soul as well as questions about the "Why?" for your mind to consider.

For some, experiences with physical angels can cause extreme sadness or confusion. Such visitors tend to come in and out of our lives very quickly. For me, such encounters, however brief, provide intuitive clues as to where to travel next on the spiritual path. This is what happened on the day I opened my front door to the two proselytizers. After our short conversation, my future course of events was forever altered. I praise their bravery for coming to my door that day, and my heart still feels gratitude for the two of them. Their bold invitation to join their religious community provided me with an example of how to stand up for my own beliefs and reach out to others within my spiritual community.

As a minister's daughter, I came to know the religious world from inside out, to recognize its collective strengths and weaknesses. I recognize the fact that the church offers the infrastructure necessary to allow many followers to remain close to God. To be part of organized religion or not is a personal choice with which each human being must come to terms at some point. Some choose to explore their spirituality outside of the church, a fact that I am aware of and accept as their choice.

For me, what is important is following the path leading toward the fullest understanding, or greater enlightenment. This means placing my complete trust in the process of God and knowing that the next step of the journey will be revealed to me as it comes. It is not always a simple path to follow, and the challenges one may encounter might be avoided along the traditional religious route.

Not everyone I meet is appreciative of my approach to religion and spirituality. Some are adamant that I pick one side or the other. My feeling is that shifting perspectives afford the greatest learning opportunities. In the case of the two people who knocked on the door of my home to ask if I had found Jesus, I might have responded by mimicking their actions and judging those who do not practice religion the "right way." However, I chose to view the experience from a different vantage point and to embrace the process of God being revealed by the visitors. On the day that the three of us came together, we were all in alignment with this process. How we chose to view it was up to each one of us. I am thankful for my perspective. Nevertheless, there are many in the religious community who hold tight to the archaic thoughts echoing those of the strangers at my door.

After being discovered as intuitively sensitive, I have occasionally been the victim of "religious bullying." I have experienced vicious name-calling and been asked to repent for my sins and the intuitive work that I do with clients. You might think that I feel anger and hatred for this type of behavior, coming as it does from so-called religious folk. While I feel personally hurt by these aspersions, I am not spiritually hurt. As an adult, I had to come to peace with the fact that certain circles of believers may not accept me. When I was younger, the desire for acceptance led me to try to abandon my intuitive gifts. Later, I recognized that the opinions of others were irrelevant in comparison with the blessings that only come from communing with your inner soul. It took a while for me to understand that the abusive words from others were the result of their human fear.

As a minister, my own father has had to grapple with my break from tradition. With the two of us unable to see eye-to-eye, the conflict put a strain on our relationship for many years. We went round and round trying to find common ground on this subject as well as peace with one another. We both have strong opinions and deep convictions for our respective points of view. His position is logical and is backed by a book to which he can refer. Mine, on the other hand, is abstract and supported only by my own inner sense of knowing.

It's difficult to articulate a point of view that originates from an experience of God rather than from an established religious paradigm. When it comes to having an interactive dialogue with spirit, there are no written rules or established procedures to follow. Soul-initiated actions are guided by the internal moral compass, which follows the eternal principals of Heaven and Earth.

I have never attempted to sway my father or my mother to my point of view. My parents dedicated their lives to their faith and to my father's career. Their lifelong, steadfast commitment to their convictions commands respect. However, I did want my parents to understand that my belief system represents an evolution from "micro-religious" thoughts to "macro-spiritual" awareness. Though we walk different paths, we are all worthy in the eyes of God. Ultimately, our love for each other is greater than our differences, and we have been able to negotiate our way to neutral ground.

I continue on my unique path while maintaining respect for organized religion. Despite the hurt I have personally experienced, I am continually reminded of the importance of the church's emphasis on structure and commitment. The spiritual path, like the religious path, requires ongoing effort. Intuitive interpretations must be continually refined to arrive at the soul's truth. While I will always be connected to my inner soul voice and the intuitive language of love, I refuse to pick a side to follow exclusively. The melting pot of experiences has provided me with an ever-increasing awareness of divine purpose. Even the passing judgments I receive from others make me more resolute in my desire to keep serving God to the best of my abilities.

Spiritual intuitive sensing aids in that process. It is a language available to all humans and does not discriminate between those of different religions, ethnicities, gender or sexual orientation. It is the common denominator of every human being alive. Though the intellectual or religious mind might try to dissect or dismiss the gift, nothing can affect the sheltered energetic soul, which is love, and the innate intuitive voice that resides within you.

Spiritual Intuitive Sensing: Cherry Picking or Communing with the Saints?

Everywhere I go, people ask me a lot of questions when they find out what I do for a living. I am a spiritual intuitive life coach. Most ignore the word "spiritual" in my career title and ask me for the "Hollywood version" of what I do. They seek intuitive information about their own lives—the entertaining aspect of my services. However, prophesying is not the focus of my work. Spiritual intuitive sensing is natural communication with your inner soul and is accessed to guide you to your highest good, not to manipulate others. The second soul lesson in Chapter 6 was structured to offer you a positive experience with this gift.

You have the capability of tapping into this abundant resource of positive energy if you do it for the right reasons. As I have explained, for a brief time during my teen years I tried to restrict the use of my intuitive communications to fit in with others. However, those efforts were pointless, and the messages rebounded stronger than ever when I tried to ignore them. Intuitive sensing was simply part of my make-up, my divine energy rhythm and the way my soul articulates with the outer world.

Staying alert to the voices and lessons that come our way helps us to grow and mature spiritually. When I was a girl sitting in church, I noticed that some parishioners would be all ears when it came to some of the sermons my father preached. Yet when certain topics were discussed, they would simply shut down and not listen at all. Their lack of commitment to stay present with every lesson offered was disheartening to me. How could they possibly know which lesson would trigger their soul to grow and expand?

The tendency to pick and choose what they wanted to hear might be called a "cherry-picking" approach to spirituality. They determined which scriptures they would abide by and which ones they would ignore. Although the instruction being given was exactly what their souls wanted them to receive, they remained impervious to the cues being offered from the universe. They were too lost in their own human dramas and had become cut off from the process of God at work in their lives.

As discussed in the second lesson, life is built around a continuum of lessons meant to keep the soul engaged in learning all the time. When you chart your divine energy rhythm in the exercise, you begin to sense when you are moving from the *being* to the *doing* phase of learning. The exercise illustrates how living in the process of God is not a stop-and-go existence but a consistent rhythm. Sometimes the lessons are more pronounced and active, while other times they are quiet and almost unnoticeable. What is significant is that you are always in the loop of lessons. When you recognize this, you move into absolute alignment with everything you are doing.

By paying close attention to your spiritual intuitive language, you will realize that each message or cue carries with it a piece of insight pertaining to the lesson at hand. The messages allow you to move through the lesson with ease and understanding. So that the information you receive is not misused, you must become clear on your intentions for committing to this type of awakened sensing. Internal checks must be done throughout the day to ensure your words and deeds are in alignment with your assignments from a higher source. Many people find they are overwhelmed or immobilized when they realize the significance of this assignment. How do you live your day-to-day life when every moment is meant to be aligned with your higher purpose? You begin by breaking it down into specific, spiritual steps.

Step One: Define Your Purpose

It is exciting to access your spiritual intuitive language. It is about tuning into both earthly and heavenly cues, interpreting them, and then translating them into cohesive thoughts and actions. The process leads to the recognition that there is a higher purpose to your existence. More important than the pure physical entertainment, soul enjoyment affords us the opportunity to experience pleasures such as spiritual bliss and unconditional love to the extent that we can in a three-dimensional world.

Connecting to your intuitive language can help you obtain a more awakened point of reference for your life, or it can simply give you cues on how to empower yourself with higher wisdom. Decide what your purpose is for connecting to this divine process. If you do not define this purpose for accessing the spiritual intuitive language, the experience will be hollow. Intuitive cues and messages will always be in alignment with your spiritual purpose. Many cues encourage you to make hard decisions about your life course or plan. For instance, you may receive a message to end a relationship that is not in the highest good for you or your significant other. Are you are willing to heed an intuitive cue suggesting that you need to make changes in your life because they are in the best spiritual interest for you and your partner? Put great thought into your motives before you take the next step of action.

STEP TWO: BECOME AN OPEN RECEIVER

Once you have opened your heart and soul to the universe, the messages or cues will become more obvious. The information that has always been waiting for you will begin to capture your full attention. You will start to recognize that the subtle presentation is a quiet sign that your spiritual intuitive language has been activated and that it is time for you to become present to the process.

You can receive as many cues or messages for yourself as you wish. While it can be rewarding to help your friends and others by sharing messages with them, it adds an entirely different aspect to the process if you choose to share what you receive. Although I offer intuitive insights for a living, I have been doing this kind of spiritual work my entire life and fully understand the ramifications of sharing intuitive insights with others. It is necessary to be very cautious about exchanging this type of information. Always keep in mind that it is the other person's life, journey and lessons to be learned. To interfere with this process is not always a good idea. If you feel the absolute need to share specific information, present it in a loving, truthful and nonjudgmental way.

The messages and cues you receive will be presented to you through your five senses in two basic ways: heavenly messages and earthly messages. Here are the basic descriptions of each type:

Heavenly Messages and Cues

These messages originate from outside our physical reality—from the *other side*. Coming from beyond the veil that separates Heaven and Earth, these signs might be considered out of the ordinary. They include symbols associated with dream states and visions received during meditation and prayer. Throughout this book, I have mentioned messages that I have received from my "angels" or guides. Angelic messages can include signs that you cannot see with the naked eye. These insights might appear as thoughts or awareness of people or other living creatures who have passed over, your guides and master teachers.

Earthly Messages and Cues

These messages are conveyed through physical realities, people, animals and the environment. They are concrete, tangible encounters and might include religious text or might appear in your doodling, artwork and writing. They include all physical signs, conversations, strange encounters and social gatherings.

Step Three: Practice Divine Timing

Messages might be received during the stage of being or the stage of doing. Either way, it is crucial that you act upon the information at the right time. Learning spiritual timing is a challenge for many. There is a tendency to want to act immediately upon every cue when doing so could result in negative consequences. Use your own good judgment in determining when to act and when to wait. Ask yourself if this message should be acted upon during the phase of doing or the phase of being. Learning to receive intuitive communications does not mean that you stop thinking rationally.

As you consider acting on any cue or message, continue to ask yourself throughout the day if you feel aligned with your assignments from a higher source. This may seem like a big assignment. However, life takes on a whole new dimension when you consider that every moment offers you an opportunity to align with your higher purpose.

STEP FOUR: PRACTICE DISCERNMENT

Though there are an endless number of messages and cues that you might identify, living in the process of God is not about acting on every single message. Some information might serve as a call to spiritual action or lead to an activity that falls into the category of the *art of doing*. However, not every message demands action; some require reflection rather than a physical response. Both types of messages will be received, and both are essential for keeping spiritual balance. It is your responsibility to discern whether the response to the message falls into the category of the *art of doing* or the *art of being*. When you begin to recognize which intuitive symbols, cues and messages categorize each phase, this discernment will become second nature to you.

It is important to note that not all the messages and cues you receive will be happy ones. To follow a spiritual path is about living in full truth, as is receiving information via intuitive sensing. The messages are meant to disclose information to help you make sound judgments. It is pointless to ask to receive only positive insights, as I discovered for myself years ago. It is important to see the whole picture and to recognize that some of God's lessons will offer challenges.

STEP FIVE: ACCEPT THE GIFT

Many authors, spiritual teachers, and personalities in the media profess a special talent for accessing intuitive communications. Some of them would suggest that they are the "chosen ones" and that this gift has somehow been bestowed into their capable hands. They might also suggest that common people are not equipped to handle the powerful energy associated with the gift.

The reality is that every one of us has the ability to receive the gift of spiritual intuitive sensing. There are, of course, differences in how individuals receive and make use of the information. Some abuse the privilege and some cannot handle the insights properly. However, everyone has the capacity to connect with his or her spiritual intuitive language. Personally, I believe everyone ought to be allowed to do so without fear of being judged by others.

While I do not consider myself the recipient of special talents, I do consider myself wise in the ways of making use of all the gifts bestowed upon me on this journey through the lessons I have received. We face so many challenges and difficult circumstances in the world today and it is all the more important to remember the spiritual context of our lives. Our spiritual intuitive language allows us to cut through man-made realities and to access the soul voice within that seeks the greater goal of peace for all.

Long ago, humans existed in a state of total alignment with their intuition and five senses—as certain indigenous people still do today. Whether hunting in the forest, sensing unseen danger or communing with spirit, all sources of knowledge were utilized. There was an unspoken awareness and respect for the sacred connection between all living creatures. Over time, "gut feelings" or intuitive connections were replaced by the sophisticated intellect. Cognitive reasoning and evolving linguistics began replacing nature's spiritual intuitive language. Humans set off on a course in which magical possibilities and limitless expectations were replaced by a belief system of rational thinking and explainable realities.

Currently, I believe the pendulum is swinging back. Many are rediscovering their own intuitive sensing and using this tool to determine what is fair, just and equitable for all humankind. They are not afraid to receive the blessings of the universe, to develop more elevated relationships with others and with God. While aware that the answers they seek lie within, they seek validation of their spiritual experience.

In this time of "second awakening," many continue to feel at home with their chosen religious practices. However, they are compelled to move beyond a myopic expression of their spirituality and advance to the next level. While they have no interest in replacing their religious views, they want to build upon the rich foundation that is already firmly in place. Many feel uncomfortable with a society fraught with separatism and exclusivity and are beginning to see the interconnectedness, the oneness of all life. This type of awareness gives rise to what I call the *pluralistic servant*. This is someone who is ready to embrace all the miracles the universe has to offer without limitations.

Becoming a pluralistic servant does not require one to scratch religion and build an entirely new spiritual system. It simply involves building upon the tools already in place in order to obtain greater clarity. I began this process when I was a child and made the decision to keep both the intuitive and religious parts of myself active. To develop this dual awareness, I have used three specific tools: prayer, meditation and spiritual intuitive sensing.

Prayer is associated with conscious intentions and is a direct reflection of our moral religious teachings. It is a ritualistic activity that follows a prescribed religious doctrine. It can be a series of rhythmic mantras or a free-flowing inner dialogue with a higher power. It is associated with the art of doing phase. Often, prayers are spoken to request an answer of some kind. I enjoy the act of praying, both individually and with a group. It calms my inner fears of being alone on this spiritual journey.

Meditation is also a ritualistic activity, but it is done without defined expectations or specific intentions. This abstract and somewhat transcendental practice is associated with the art of being. It offers time-out to quiet the mind, body and soul and helps you to remain peaceful among the chaos. This kind of activity encourages you to search for answers from within rather than from outside sources.

I have come to depend on meditation since I was a child, though I didn't even know the appropriate name for it at the time. It takes time and practice to calm the mind chatter and accept the experience, but the rewards are worth the effort. The overwhelming sense of oneness with God grows stronger with each session.

Two distinct practices, both prayer and meditation, are commonplace in the practice of religious and spiritual teachings. While meditation offers a peaceful state of mind, it is next to impossible to participate fully in the world while engaged in this state of being. Prayer, likewise, is an activity usually done intermittently, though often on a regular basis. After questions are posed, one continues on, frequently without immediate answers. It is spiritual intuitive sensing that allows one to live in the world while remaining continuously connected to the process of God and to receive the answers for which one is searching.

Spiritual intuitive sensing incorporates cues from both heavenly and earthly sources and gives voice to the religious ideologies we hold in high esteem. It is precisely through this language that one "hears" or recognizes core values and beliefs. Such information is conveyed through sight, sound, touch, taste and scent and brings beliefs to action. The messages you have received and assimilated determine how you act in the world when no one is looking.

While there tends to be a serious undertone to religion and spirituality in general, some aspects of developing our souls can be *fun*. Spiritual intuitive sensing is the resource that affords the opportunity to savor every moment. It is not just about receiving and acting out messages and cues from Heaven and Earth. Sometimes subtle messages and cues might encourage you to do something out of the ordinary, or something you think might be inappropriate for a religious practitioner. However, if you are willing to risk momentary awkwardness, you might gain the rewards of intensely beautiful emotions and experiences. If you feel the energy of God rushing to your feet and find it difficult to contain yourself, let loose and dance in the streets. When you're having coffee with your dearest friend and you sense the urge to grab her in a big bear hug, just do it! Spiritual intuitive sensing is about breaking through religious inhibitions and claiming the way of the soul with gusto.

When learning to live an awakened existence and to use these forms of spiritual communication, it is necessary to remain objective and keep an eye on your internal growth and progress at all times. At some point, you might find that your intuitive messages or cues may be in direct disagreement with the intellect. You will then have to negotiate with your intellect (earthly decisions) and your intuitive sensing (heavenly) to come to some kind of resolution. It is your responsibility to process both types of messages in order to determine the appropriate action. This task requires careful discernment and practice.

In the next chapter, I explore the intuitive messages you receive from all five of your senses. Both heavenly and earthly cues will be examined and you will learn to follow through on this information with awakened action.

9

THIRD SOUL LESSON

Expanding Your Intuitive Language

In the second soul lesson you began to create your "Spiritual Intuitive Handbook." In it, you were asked to record spontaneous messages and cues, material that came to your mind. You were to record these without adding any conscious effort. The hope is that you learned it is possible to receive messages and cues via spiritual intuitive sensing without making any exaggerated efforts. Spiritual intuitive language is an energetic linguistic system continuously transmitting millions of heavenly and earthly messages. Your five senses process this soul work without your knowledge. The next step is to apply your conscious awareness to the messages you have received and to become more interactive with this automatic spiritual system.

EXERCISE ONE

STEP ONE: THE GATHERING STAGE

Please refer to your first entries from the second soul lesson in Chapter 6. You should have listed the intuitive conscious messages and cues that you gathered when you were charting your divine energy rhythm. As discussed, all intuitive messages and cues derive from either a heavenly source or an earthly source. To become comfortable with these categories, go back and be sure all your entries are labeled as either heavenly (having been received during the art of being) or earthly (having been received during the art of doing). In this way you will see where you tend to focus most of your energy.

Next, divide the remainder of your notebook into five sections and label each section with a separate sense. Placing tabs on the side will help you access each category easily. You can, of course, design the book however it works best for you. Once you've organized your notebook, you are ready to develop your own spiritual intuitive language from the messages and cues you have recorded.

Do not worry if you have not recorded a great number of messages. Just continue to remain aware as you carry on with your normal routine. Realize that you will receive any messages you are meant to hear. Practice will increase your rewards here. If you are extremely analytical in your thinking (bottom heavy), and spend most of your time in the act of doing, it may take some effort to tune in to your intuitive language. On the other hand, if you are top heavy and spend most of your time in the art of being, you may need to assert more effort when it comes to following through with the messages you have received.

STEP TWO: DETERMINE THROUGH WHICH OF THE SENSES YOUR CUES WERE PERCEIVED

As you begin to categorize your messages by sense, you will see that like all other physical senses, one in particular may show a tendency toward dominance. This is not unusual and only becomes an issue if you always overlook the other senses. Certain messages and cues can only be broadcast through a specific sense. If that sense is shut down, you may not be receiving the full advantage of the intuitive language system. For instance, the sense of smell plays an essential role in many ceremonies and brings forth special messages that can only be received if you include this sense in the process.

Each of our five senses offers unique information to help us move along our spiritual paths. The following pages explain specific content, material that can be received via intuitive language. Exercises are provided after the explanation of each intuitive sense. Complete each exercise and record your results in your handbook.

The Sense of Sight

Heavenly Messages

When it comes to intuitive messages, people are perhaps most familiar with content being received via the sense of sight. Artists and filmmakers have sometimes depicted how spiritual energy might appear. Many are fascinated by the ability to "see" invisible energy from the other side.

Many sacred and ancient texts have offered the concept there is a living life force within every living creature. Only after death does this life force dissipate. The energy gives off a specific color hue that surrounds the entire physical body. As a result, this creates a transparent halo effect, akin to what I observed when I was a young girl—and in particular what I observed around both the church elders and the older woman who was passing over, as I explained in Chapter Four. Their colors transmitted a hue that could be seen by anyone who was in tune with their spiritual intuitive sensing. Colors provide information about the state of the soul and can assist you in communicating with others physically as well as spiritually.

Many individuals have this gift of intuitive sight but shy away from using it because it is in conflict with their belief system. Others may have noticed the effect but do not trust what they see and second-guess themselves. Nonetheless, this is the one gift I wish I could give anyone who desires the blessing because it permits one to see an added dimension of beauty in our planet. The colors are truly spectacular—sometimes almost too much for the naked eye to take in. The variable palette reveals information about the soul that can only been seen through the intuitive sensing color. It permits you to access the world of "unspoken spiritual body language."

Some are afraid of asking for this gift because they fear what they might see in others. If you detach from this fear, you will discover that intuitive sight can be an effective and useful assessment tool. You will be amazed how helpful it can be. The world is made up of all kinds of people with a variety of intentions—some healthy and some not so healthy. By using the tool of intuitive color sensing, you can become aware of these intentions.

There is no way to change or alter the heavenly auras bestowed on all living entities. I found this out over the course of seeing thousands of colors around those I encounter. Over the course of this discovery, I have identified two distinct color rings. They are denoted as the primary base color ring and secondary base color ring, as illustrated in figure three.

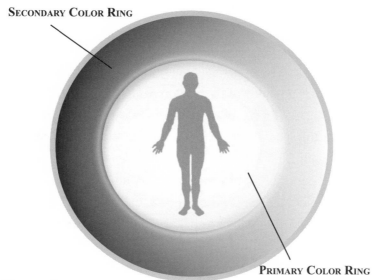

SECONDARY COLOR RING

PRIMARY COLOR RING

FIGURE 3

The primary color ring or band appears as a diffused silhouette closest to the physical body structure and extends about six inches out in all directions. It represents the original soul color you receive at birth. This color hue is static by nature, which means the color will not change over the course of a lifetime. Reflecting the specific soul lesson each person was born to learn, the color represents the recurring theme of a human's life. This constant, though often unseen, feature is a manifestation of the lessons that are being repeatedly experienced. You cannot physically will your primary base color to change. It identifies who you are spiritually and offers hints on how to prepare for your soul lessons, which invariably relate to the experience of Godly, unconditional love.

Throughout my practice, many have asked me if I have ever seen a base color of black around anyone. They no doubt assume that the color black represents evil. However, I can say without hesitation that up this point in my lifetime, I have observed this in no one. However, black does sometimes appear as a secondary color band. You can read my definition of black in the upcoming section, "Secondary Band Color Index."

Below is an index of base colors with their associated soul lessons. Each color represents a theme for a particular life journey. Use this guideline and try to see how it applies to your specific path. The list I have created is subjective and is only a starting point for you to work from. Read over the list when you are quiet and see if you can pick up any cues that might help you discern which category or color resonates with you. As you become familiar with your own intuitive language, you may add additional meanings or even change the meanings to reflect what the colors mean to you personally.

PRIMARY BAND COLOR INDEX

Red: You are here to experience the unconditional physical love found in human relationships. Spiritual love is already understood.

Orange: You are here to experience unconditional physical and spiritual love for yourself.

Yellow: You are here to experience unconditional physical love and spiritual love through the experience of participating in groups.

Green: You are here to experience the interconnectedness of unconditional love working through all people.

Blue: You are here to communicate and teach others about the essence of unconditional love.

Violet: You are here to sense intuitively and experience unconditional love in all living beings.

White: You are here to sense intuitively the core essence of God, spiritual enlightenment, and tutor others in this message. This color can also contain intermittent flecks of metallic gold and silver, which denote the highest level of understanding and communing with the God source.

Pink: You are here to experience the true embodiment of unconditional love as it is manifested on the planet.

Brown: You are here to experience all aspects of a deep relationship between yourself and planet Earth.

Everyone will experience lessons from every category, but there will be one category that applies to you overall. Pay attention to the soul lessons denoted by this particular color. An awareness of the color provides answers that you must learn before you can advance to higher soul lessons within your base color ring.

THE SECONDARY BAND

The second band of color that can be sensed is positioned just above the primary base halo. The color hue is dynamic in its color formations and changes throughout our lives. Many times people mistake this ring as the primary color band because it can overshadow the primary band. To the untrained intuitive eye, this is an easy oversight. In order to get an accurate assessment, the two distinct colors have to be discerned. The second band represents what soul lesson one is dealing with at any specific moment in time and the color reflects the lessons at hand. It provides a valuable indicator of what is truly going on in someone's life at any given time. It can change color hue from moment to moment, day to day, month to month or even year to year. Reflection on recent circumstances can provide clues to what issues or relationships are being experienced.

By perceiving another person's secondary color band, you can adjust your words or actions to fit his or her state of mind. By knowing what others need—whether it be spiritual compassion, empathy or even a little tough love—you can assist in their healing and aid their growth.

SECONDARY BAND COLOR INDEX

Red: The color red represents those circumstances associated with grounding oneself in physical surroundings, such as relocating or finding housing. When this color band is present, emotions can move from one extreme to the other, from anger to excitement, depending on outside circumstances.

Orange: The color orange is seen in those who are searching to find their true identities in the world and to discover who they are physically, spiritually or mentally.

Yellow: The color yellow is associated with finding identity within a group setting while maintaining your individuality in the world.

Green: The color green appears when one is searching for higher unconditional love in all aspects of life. It signifies trouble dealing with the unfairness of love in the world.

Blue: The color blue suggests a struggle to speak one's unconditional truth in a conditional world. It is associated with holding in words for fear of punishment.

Violet: The color violet is seen in those who are struggling to keep their intuitive sensing abilities under control. They may be avoiding intuitive messages and cues that are breaking through to their conscious thoughts.

White: The color white is associated with human beings who are experiencing momentary enlightenment or embracing the full essence of God inwardly. This state might be achieved while meditating, sitting with enlightened mentors or receiving a lesson of profound illumination.

When someone is passing over from this life into the afterlife, the entire color ring—both primary and secondary bands—eventually fades from all colors into a muted shade of opaque white.

Pink: The color pink encircles those who are in love with the world. This state might be a result of the people they are surrounded by, or it might be a result of being in a particular environment. It is the color that reflects being in love with life.

Brown: The color brown is associated with human beings who play an essential role in helping to heal the planet Earth and to maintain a healthy balance between all living creatures.

Black: The color black is visible when the soul has lost its sense of purpose and is failing to connect to its higher lessons.

Gray: The color gray appears when one is only in and out of soul lessons. These individuals do what is necessary to achieve success or their end purpose. They do not generally choose a side but rather move to the side serving their immediate physical needs.

Regarding black rings and gray rings in various shades, people who manifest these colors sometimes appear to be lacking good intentions. If they are engaging in questionable activities and show a lack of higher spiritual morals, this kind of dark essence can be reflected to others. There are people who find it difficult to follow the natural order of the love and lessons available to them. However, the good news is this color ring is subject to change if spiritual work is done and a decision is made to engage in lessons and make healthy soul choices.

Exercise Two: Asking for the Gift

If you aspire to enjoy the benefits of intuitive sight, or any of the following intuitive gifts, your first action is to ask, through meditation or prayer, that this gift be restored to you. Recognize that it will only be given if you have the highest honor and respect for this spiritual intuitive tool.

Exercise Three: Seeing Colors

Every person is unique in the way they will see energetic colors. Some may actually be able to recognize with ease the colors surrounding people and other living objects. Others may only be able to sense the color when they become particularly mindful. The way you obtain the intuitive insight is irrelevant. The point is to remain open and learn to trust your own way of tuning in to the energy.

One of the most effective ways of sensing color is by first turning away from the object you want to sense intuitively. Simply close your eyes for a brief moment and then refocus your vision on the object you have chosen. You may or may not be able to see the color, but you will instantly pick up the intuitive message or cue represented by the color. The more you do this activity the more you will strengthen the bond between your mind's eye and your intuitive sensing system.

When you first try this exercise, you may find that

you are seeing several colors at once. This might mean you are actually picking up on both color rings at the same time, which is a very positive result. Over time, you will be able to separate out the colors you are seeing. You will also begin to develop your own descriptions for the life stages associated with each color.

EARTHLY MESSAGES RECEIVED THROUGH THE SENSE OF SIGHT

For most of us, vision is the dominant sense. We take in what we see first and use our other senses later. It is impossible to list all the physical ways our sight can give us intuitive cues and messages. There are countless images you can take in each day, let alone in a lifetime.

It is often helpful to pay special attention to those items you catch in your peripheral vision. There may be a hidden meaning behind their subtle appearance. Try to notice if there is symbolic meaning for you in the objects within your area of sight. At other times, a new person might stumble into your path. If so, try to stop and be present to the individual you are seeing. Messages in the form of people are often obvious, as they tend to present themselves in a manner that is hard to miss. Listen closely to the words they are saying. They may very well be your physical angels coming to pay a visit and offering you the message you need to hear.

It bears mentioning that animals can offer other visual cues. They are closely connected to the spiritual path we walk, as I observed the day I took a walk in the woods with a close friend. As we were walking and talking I noticed, out of the corner of my eye, something running our way. Simultaneously we both made eye contact with the object: it was a red fox running straight towards us. Apparently stunned by his proximity to two human beings, the fox came within ten feet of us before darting back into the forest.

Each breed of animal embodies its particular symbolic wisdom, which the Native Americans understood. When I returned home after the "chance meeting" with the fox, I immediately recorded the encounter. These types of natural incidents can offer experiential intuitive wisdom that affects us in a way that lies outside the teaching of religious texts. They remind us of our connection to the natural world and all life on the planet.

EXERCISE FOUR: AN ALTERNATIVE EXERCISE

Although everyone has the ability to see nonphysical color hues around people, not everyone feels comfortable allowing themselves to experience these phenomenas. In that case, you may wish to try an alternative exercise.

Rather than looking for hues around living people, simple assess the colors you see on a day-to-day basis. Notice the colors in homes as well as the colors of people's clothing and symbolic artifacts. Apply the same principles of intuitive energy sensing to the physical colors you see. Even this seemingly obvious information provides cues about others and your environment to assist in your growth and understanding. Colors, both physical and nonphysical, have a language.

Record your findings in your handbook and refer to the same index provided in the Heavenly cues for spiritual insights when interpreting the physical colors.

THE SENSE OF TASTE

HEAVENLY MESSAGES

You might not think to associate the sense of taste with your intuition. However, it can be a powerful intuitive sense, one that offers unique insights. Through the centuries and across cultures, the preparation of meals has been a ritual activity that has essentially been the domain of women. They understand the important relationship between humans and the food they eat, and women intuitively understand the vibrational energy resonating within all living plants and animals. The preparation of the meal is just as sacred as the food they will serve. In some cultures, women sing or chant sacred song verses while they chop and cook. The energy goes directly from their voices straight into the food source. In a way, their spiritual love for others and for their higher source is absorbed into the meal itself.

You have all have experienced food in this way, though perhaps without even realizing it. Think about the last time you made a special dinner for your loved ones. You might have been singing or humming love songs and sending unconscious vibrations into the food as you prepared it. Alternatively, you might have eaten after having an argument with someone and the food was prepared from the energy of anger and sadness. Consider this the next time you have the opportunity to prepare a meal for another. How is your spiritual energy affecting the other person's sense of taste? The choice is yours.

EARTHLY MESSAGES FROM THE SENSE OF TASTE

Many religions celebrate the embodiment of God within their sacramental rituals. Bread and juice or wine is offered to church attendees during Christian services. To those of the Christian faith, the bread represents the body of Christ and the wine or juice represents the blood of Christ. Those of the Roman Catholic faith interpret the sacraments literally.

This time-honored ritual, experienced day after day or week after week, could easily become rote. If communion is part of your worship experience, you might take time to reconsider this sacred exchange. Pause and give yourself permission to feel the energy emanating from both the bread and the wine. It may take on a completely new perspective of forgiveness and grace.

EXERCISE FIVE: THE ENERGY OF FOOD

Pay close attention to what you are eating. Can you "taste" the energy of the food you are digesting? Does it taste differently if you know the one who prepared the meal was filled with the energy of love?

Many of the foods that Americans consume these days are packaged and processed "dead foods." They do not contain any vibrational energy whatsoever. On the other hand, there is a reason why people call certain kinds of meals *soul food*—you can taste the love vibration down to the last bite. The next time you prepare a meal for yourself or your family, try praying over the food while you make it rather than only before you eat it.

SENSE OF SMELL

HEAVENLY AND EARTHLY MESSAGES

My first experience with this type of intuitive sensing message occurred when I visited a Greek Orthodox church. It was one of the first times I had attended a worship service outside of my home church. Their use of sacred incense immediately caught my attention. At first whiff, I could feel the spiritual energy churning inside my soul. The divine energy I always felt at my own church now permeated this sanctuary as well. This scent allowed my mind to transcend the difference in worship space to experience a state of quiet being.

Stimulating the sense of scent should be part of everyone's meditative practice on a regular basis. Candles, incense, oils, and flowers can trigger the mind in so many fascinating ways. Though the scent itself does not deliver a message, it sets up the mind, body and soul to receive a message or cue from the state of being. The perfume can truly transport you on a journey inward to a place of profound insights that you might not otherwise discover.

EXERCISE SIX: SCENT MEMORIES

Think back to your past, to a time when a pleasant scent evoked a reaction within you. You have probably heard that the scent of baking bread triggers a response of feeling at home or being loved, for example. If you cannot recall a scent-related memory, create a new memory. I happen to enjoy the scent of burning sage, which brings to mind fond memories of sacred exchanges with my fellow soul sisters.

Once you identify your sacred scent, meditate while breathing it in and see what happens. Remember to record your scent-related messages and cues in your handbook. These are extremely important intuitive language symbols.

KINETIC SENSE OF TOUCH

HEAVENLY MESSAGES

Heavenly sent "kinetic" messages require a high level of trust to be accepted, in comparison to the other senses. They require you to feel the energy or to sense something around you. These messages are what some refer to as "gut feelings." Unlike the messages sent via the other senses, kinetic messages are difficult to pin down in words; they just are.

The dream state, which I believe conveys spiritual intuitive language to us, can impart these types of messages. Our waking minds are overflowing with unconscious messages and cues that carry essential knowledge but have not yet been processed. If you do not allow time for meditation or quiet reflection during the day, these messages will enter your consciousness as you sleep and fill your dreams with all sorts of symbolic messages.

EXERCISE SEVEN: REVIEW YOUR DREAMS

The information we receive during our dream states can be very relevant to our spiritual growth. The dreams are not in physical form and must be intellectually recalled upon waking. These thought forms are symbolic representations of intuitive language that is being conveyed to the unconscious mind. First thing after awakening, it helps to review our dreams and extract as much pure information as possible from this kind of intuitive language (without adding additional information to fill in any memory gaps). If the image or message is not complete but is important, your unconscious mind will bring it to you again, later. Therefore, it is a good idea to write down exactly what you remember upon waking and let the blurrier images go.

Many wonderful books provide interpretations to the symbols and messages received during the dream state. It would be redundant for me to create a dream dictionary in this book. Furthermore, I believe the key to interpreting the images from your dreams resides within your soul memory banks. To find the key to one of your dreams, pose a few questions: What does this image mean for me? How do I feel about this image or object? Also consider how the message applies to your life in the present moment. This might not seem like as much fun as reading a dream dictionary, but the exercise helps to unveil your own spiritual intuitive language system.

EARTHLY KINETIC MESSAGES

Some of my favorite hidden intuitive treasures are earthly kinetic messages. The most common example of this form of soul communication is the practice of doodling. This type of drawing is a wonderful way to get in touch with your unconscious mind while you're wide-awake. It's a simple type of art therapy and can assist in your healing. Through this form of daydreaming, the soul's thoughts can be conveyed.

To help you get started as you interpret your own doodling, consider the following shapes and their suggested meanings.

Arrows: Are they pointing up or down? Upward arrows suggest upward or forward movement. Downward arrows suggest downward or backward movement. Horizontal arrows suggest neither, but rather a holding pattern in your life.

Stars: Count how many points are on the stars. Each point of the star represents either someone or some event that requires your consideration. Partial or complete shading in your stars suggests that someone or something is holding secrets.

Circles: Circles represent someone or something being added to your life. Are these circles drawn one over another? This suggests you are going in circles on your path. Half circles imply that something is stopping you from completing a task. Ask yourself what task you are avoiding.

Squares: This usually denotes a sense of being boxed in by a person or circumstance.

Written Words: Doodled words bear their literal meaning. Look for where you placed the words on the page. Are they enclosed in a particular shape? Have you repeatedly written your name or someone else's name?

Trees: Running parallel from heaven to earth, trees represent various aspects of life. Does your tree doodle look healthy, thriving, and full of leaves, or is it leafless with empty branches? If your tree stands alone on the page, it suggests that you are dealing with something that is isolating you from others *or* that you have chosen to isolate yourself in order to seek answers within. If your tree is barren and isolated, observe the other doodles on the page. A tree is very rarely dying in the forest alone. Consider what you might have created to cause others to leave your life.

If your tree is dead, go back to the doodle and sketch in new elements. Add leaves to the branches and plants at the base to represent renewal in your life. Are there any birds in the trees?

Birds: Perched up high or flying above, birds represent complete freedom. They also represent people in most cases. If the birds are in a tree, how many are there? Does one of the birds in a dead tree represent you trying to fly away from your troubles? Alternatively, a bird in a healthy tree might suggest that you are ready to take flight into your next adventure.

Hearts: The heart, of course, is the universal symbol for love in any language. It is one of the first shapes a child learns to cut and paste in kindergarten. However, it can also represent complications or even heartache in certain doodles.

Multiple hearts: Repeated hearts denote one who loves many. Larger hearts can represent the significant other in your life while smaller hearts represent love of parents, siblings, children or others. Sometimes multiple hearts represent the decision that must be made in choosing one love over another.

Overlapping hearts: These hearts suggest love with complications. When does one relationship end and another begin?

Also look for other significant symbols—arrows, names or shading—drawn together with the hearts. Evaluate the meaning of each separate symbol to discover the entire intuitive message. Redraw any overlapping hearts as separate images and consider whether they represent someone. Ask yourself how you feel about each love of your life individually.

XXXXXX: X marks the spot, literally! This common symbol, which is used in every day communication, takes on a new meaning when doodled in our unconscious drawings. When used to cross out names or drawn over a heart or other symbol, it can represent danger to another. Always take notice of any Xs in your drawings and, for that matter, anyone else's drawings.

Partial shading of symbols: Shading of various shapes or symbols suggests how open (not shaded) or closed (shaded) one is to the kinetic intuitive messages coming through doodling.

Complete dark shading of symbols: This type of shading suggests a refusal to look beyond both conscious and unconscious messages. The message is cut off just as it breaks through the physical plane. Ask yourself what is hiding behind the dark shadows.

Polka dots: These represent spaces that allow communication between the conscious and the unconscious worlds. You are able to receive messages from the heavenly realm if you look closely.

Note that there are some people who never doodle. If you happen to be one of these, it simply means that you do not receive intuitive messages through this particular sense. Look to the other senses to develop your intuitive communication.

Exercise Eight: Working with Doodles

Start this exercise with the doodles you have already created in the past. Try to evaluate honestly what you see on paper. Use the list I provide to begin assessing your creations. Look for repeated patterns in symbols, words, or messages. They will show trends of which you may or may not be aware.

Now take out your spiritual intuitive handbook and select any one of the sense categories. Begin doodling on one of the pages. It makes no difference where you do this exercise in the handbook. Half the fun is asking your intuitive soul voice which category you should start with. *Do not* give conscious thought or attention to what you are drawing when you are doing this activity. Let your creative unconscious imagination go free.

After you have completed your drawing, you can go back, evaluate, and even adjust the content. For example, if you are seeing patterns of downward arrows, go back and draw your arrows in an upward position instead. If you are drawing incomplete circles, return to them and finish them properly. This nonverbal language will speak to the soul, sending a message of renewed conviction that you want to move forward on the spiritual path.

SENSE OF SOUND

Lastly, there is the sense of sound—the second most commonly received type of message. Sounds can be most subtle in their presentation. This is an interactive sense and often presents as conversation.

It is very important to clarify exactly what it means to "hear" spiritual messages and cues. Hearing voices in your head is associated with mental illness and is not what I am referring to. You should also bear in mind that authentic spiritual intuitive messages do not contain negative thoughts or suggest negative behavior, such as encouraging you to hurt yourself or others. If you experience anything of this nature, you should seek professional help immediately.

HEAVENLY AND EARTHLY MESSAGES AND CUES FROM THE SENSE OF SOUND

As with the sense of sight, messages from the sense of sound bombard us on a daily basis. It is, however, a challenge to separate these types of messages into heavenly and earthly categories, as was done with the sense of sight. Whether sent from the physical or heavenly realm, oratory messages are interwoven into our day during both the art of doing and the art of being. The information sent is constantly in line with our activity at hand and can offer a valuable tool for making last-minute decisions.

There have been numerous instances where someone "heard" a silent message to run away from a situation, one that turned out to be dangerous or life-threatening. Physical angels can also appear and speak aloud to you, offering the exact information you need to hear to solve a problem. Because of its subtle presentation, we miss many intuitive cues from the sense of sound. Learning to be a good listener helps you to develop this intuitive sense.

EXERCISE NINE: LISTENING TO WHISPERS

The best way to discover intuitive messages from the sense of sound is to be patient and wait for the information to present itself in its whispering ways. This intuitive sense will strengthen though trial and error. When you hear a message, follow through with what you are called to do. Carry out the instructions with as little resistance on your part as possible. Oratory messages tend to relate to lessons being experienced the moment the message is received. If you choose to ignore the message, it may affect you in pronounced ways down the road. Of all the senses, it is especially important that you make an effort to become aware of these messages and cues and record them in your handbook consistently. Eventually, you will develop an automatic awareness of the subtle presentation.

Follow Through

Receiving messages from spirits is the fun part of working with your spiritual intuitive language. However, it is not sufficient simply to wish or think the messages into reality. Like all worthy rewards, work must be done in order to accomplish the goal. The messages must be interpreted correctly, and concrete actions must follow. Let us consider that you have completed all the sensing exercises in this chapter. In this case, you now have a fair amount of entries in each category. You can now review your content and consider acting upon the messages you have received.

While we live in a world where time is linear, intuitive messages do not always have to be acted upon immediately after they are received. To determine when it is time to act, become aware of your divine energy rhythm. Whether you are engaged in the art of being or the art of doing, your soul's desires are in balance with the lessons at hand. Use your best judgment to determine which messages should be acted upon and in which phase in order to achieve the best result.

It is very possible that you will encounter intuitive information that you will not want to act upon. In this case, remember that there are no right or wrong choices or spiritual consequences. You can simply refuse to follow intuitive information. However, if you are seeking new results in life, then it will serve you to accept the intuitive choice that has been given. Learn to trust your "gut" and go for it.

10

Journey to the East

A lthough I have been working as an intuitive life coach for
some years now, there was a time when I was searching to
define my own spiritual path. After graduating from high
school, I felt ready to move beyond my home church experience,
to spread my wings and explore areas outside our denomination.
I yearned to connect with a community of like-minded individuals who were seeking to live a more awakened existence. I had no
idea where I might find such a community, or if it even existed.

As it turned out, I did not have to venture too far from
familiar territory to find the opportunity I sought. I enrolled
in a Christian liberal arts college located in a small rural community; this turned out to be the perfect place for my internal
spiritual life to blossom without outside interference.

As a young adult I continued to receive intuitive messages, although the angelic encounters were not as pronounced
as they had been when I was a child. Having passed through

the period during adolescence when I tried to suppress my intuitive nature, I had learned to go with the flow and take the appropriate action when messages came through to me. The information I received from my guides was sometimes so subtle that I would periodically do a "spirit check" to be sure they were still nearby. I would pause for a moment to see if I could still "feel" the energies in close proximity—thankfully I continued to sense their presence. In time, the intuitive information I received became naturally integrated into my daily routine and operated as a unified internal mechanism. This practice led to my current way of life.

In my new environment at college, I found I was suddenly free to choose my own friends, whereas most of my friends until that point—young members of my father's church—had been essentially chosen for me. Now I was able to decide for myself what I was looking for in a friend. I felt rather naïve as a college freshman and unsure of how to begin the process of establishing a new social circle. I was also surprised to discover that even though my new college was affiliated with a specific Christian faith, the student population was a mix of many religious denominations. For the first time, friendships could be formed on the basis of someone's soul rather than their religion!

It was a relief in many ways to be set free from the religious golden cage and to leave behind my role in "American spiritual royalty." However, I did find myself among a number of other preachers' kids. We had all experienced the same privileges growing up behind our parents' protective robes; now it was time to make our way in the world on our own merits.

Preachers' kids often find themselves going in one of two opposing directions when they grow up: they either go either completely off the deep end, often abusing drugs and alcohol to cope with the pressure to be perfect, or they emulate the lifestyle they were raised in and become ministers themselves. I was inclined to neither of these choices.

Though many of my close friends thought I would become a minister, I eventually decided that this was not a profession for which I was suited. There were moments when I had contemplated this career path, though. While I knew the sacrifices involved, the ministry was a lifestyle that I understood and a calling that celebrated the love of God and provided an opportunity to serve in it.

During childhood, the cookie-cutter mold of religious practices came into conflict with my wildly adventurous spiritual connections with the other side. After being tested to the limits, these connections proved unbreakable. It seemed impossible for me to become part of a system that had nearly extinguished the free spirit within me and would possibly do the same to the next generation of awakened children. Though I felt this could not be my calling or destiny, I felt a strong desire to serve in some kind of spiritual capacity. As I contemplated my choices, I deliberately took a hiatus from my religious practice to step back and regroup. The environment at college afforded me the freedom to do so.

Growing up, it had been a rarity to miss Sunday church service; it was our family's routine as well as obligation and thus something we honored without fail. But when I had the chance to break the habit, I did so immediately. The only problem was that I could not shake off the Sunday morning guilt. Still viewing church as a duty, I would attend with my friends once in a while. Not going to church would literally make me sick to my stomach with shame, though it was shame for failing to support an institution that encouraged religious, cultural and sexual separatism.

As I came to recognize that I had dedicated so much effort to evolving past the limited archaic religious thinking I had witnessed growing up, I ultimately decided that I could not attend church merely to please others. I was still trying to define myself spiritually and was befriending incredible people from diverse religious backgrounds; I wanted to explore these new connections and felt that I could return to church only when doing so came into accordance with my spiritual heart. Until then, I would have to battle my insecurities and guilt.

I could have easily sold out, sacrificed everything I had fought for up to this point and abandoned my spiritual exploration. Thankfully, I received one last intense message from the other side, a message that served to carry me forward on the journey through adulthood. The words from my guides sent on a winter night provided me with the assurance that I was indeed on the right professional and spiritual path.

I was making my way back to my dorm room through biting winds, when a familiar booming male voice broke through the darkness. The message contained the answer to the question I had been asking myself since I arrived at school. Namely, did I have to take the traditional route and become a minister as everyone expected me to do? I heard a resounding *No!* The message expressed in detail how the church, spirituality and religion would adopt a more worldly perspective by the time I was ready to begin my chosen work in the world.

> The world's religious and spiritual institutions will become synonymous with the universal word of God and love. All religious orders will be availed the opportunity to join spiritual world neutrality only if they can overcome their prejudices to do so.

> We are willing to let you break free from your Christian faith *but* in return, you must promise today that you will be a part of the worldly transition as it unfolds in the future.

I was being asked to make a commitment to be involved in the universal shift that would take place during my adulthood. It seemed like a reasonable request and as it turns out, it was one that I would eventually be able to fulfill. Without really considering what I was acquiescing to, I accepted this spiritual commitment. As a college kid living in the moment, I simply filed away the promise, which I would then forget until destiny called me into willing servitude years later.

From this point, my life progressed along a typical course for a time. I finished college, earning a degree in psychology, then I entered the workforce, married and started a family. Lingering in the back of my mind was the memory of my break with the church as well as the promise I made to my guides during college. I didn't worry too much about it and told myself everything would work out in time.

My career path turned out to be a combination of what I

consider destiny and free will choices. However explained, it has been a path of exciting twists and turns. After graduating from college, I became involved in the modeling and beauty industry. In order to advance in this career field, I returned to school and became a licensed aesthetician. I had a dream of opening a day spa and wellness center, and with sheer will and determination I did just that. The spa was the perfect setting to express my creative ideas and to develop my intuitive sensing abilities.

Before that time, the intuitive messages I had received were directed to me personally. This pattern changed entirely when I was providing aesthetic services to a woman who happened to have intuitive abilities as well. During our intermittent conversations, we somehow started discussing the subject of spirituality. She was quite open about her own abilities to sense messages from the other side and described almost verbatim what I had been experiencing since childhood. Further, like me, this woman had a traditional religious upbringing and had been left to make sense of her spiritual encounters alone. As I listened to her speak, I could hardly contain myself and focus on the work at hand. She went on to explain there were other spiritually minded people in her inner circle.

At the end of our session together, something memorable occurred: the treatment room became populated with her angels from the other side as well as my angels. I could sense hesitation on the part of my angels. They appeared to be questioning my intentions, though I was doing nothing more than giving a facial! My client was aware enough to know the guides were present and to sense their caution. After the tension in the room dissipated, I was able to intuitively connect and "hear" why they had come: they had brought messages for the woman, messages she needed to hear. The client gave me permission to share whatever information was being broadcast. Without skipping a beat after she spoke, the words started escaping my mouth and into her ears. This was the first of many "special deal facials" to come.

When she was leaving the treatment room, the client invited me to one of her spiritual gatherings. I accepted the offer, not knowing what I would find. If others were experiencing spiritual bliss through unconventional methods, I was curious to learn more.

A couple of weeks later I made my way to her gathering with mixed feelings, wondering what "kooky ideas" I might encounter. Perhaps these people would be oddly dressed or say strange things. My palms were sweaty but I followed my gut and continued on my way. On arrival, however, my first reaction was almost disappointment. These people looked just like me—happy and joyful to be in the company of other spiritually awakened souls. They were not dressed in outrageous getups or saying anything out of the ordinary. As I surveyed the room and took in the small talk, a benevolent looking woman approached me.

Staring deep into my brown eyes, she declared that she knew who I was. I responded politely, saying that it must be a case of mistaken identity because we had not met before. The woman replied, "No, you are an awakened intuitive who has been receiving messages since childhood but you didn't want anyone to know."

I laughed nervously, recognizing that at one fell swoop this stranger had decisively put an end to my years-long habit of hiding my intuitive sensing abilities from others when in public. Without warning, my veil of safety was taken away and I stood intuitively naked in front of her and everyone else in attendance. Once I was able to regain my composure, we spent the rest of the evening engaged in a long intimate conversation about spiritual matters. Our talk confirmed in my mind that I was on the right track with my own exploration and that the lessons I had received from my guides were parallel to what others had been learning.

The woman who had recognized me when I arrived explained the concept of a "spiritual hierarchy," one in which spiritual insights are passed from generation to generation, by word of mouth, from master teacher to student. I understood that this form of teaching was what I needed in order to progress in understanding and to achieve the next level of abundance, joy and inner peace in my life. That day I had found what I needed: my first awakened teacher. Perhaps I ought to say we found each other that day.

The experience brought to mind the two Bible-carrying men who had knocked on the door of my home years before when I was a girl. After they had asked me to tell them the date I had been saved, I'd been dismayed that I didn't know when this special date was. In reality, what I had been seeking more than a "saved date" was an "awakened date." This celebratory date in my spiritual history was September 16, 1996—the day I found my first master teacher.

After this meeting, I continued working at the spa, which

evolved into a place of healing and welcome to those who chose to visit, people from all walks of life. It offered a setting where those who were wounded and needed to surrender pain could come and share stories without fear. The meditation room was filled with sitting pillows and candles; incense burned while prayers of thanksgiving were spoken. People began coming from miles and miles around. City folk, executives from large, well-known companies, and working moms with their children discovered our place hidden in the hills and rejuvenated their souls. Some people came to experience the energy and healing while others came for basic spa services. But the word quickly spread about my "special facials," for they combined a standard facial with angel communication. Only given on request, this special service was identified by a unique "code word" known only to the staff and me.

At the day spa and wellness center, the agreement I had made with the angels back in college was coming to fruition. The business I had started was transforming into a healing and spiritual education facility. The experience afforded me the opportunity to work in the trenches—with my invisible workforce at my side—to assist those who were in need. Although working in the ministry might have offered similar opportunities, I felt that working in the spa offered a real world experience where an array of people from a wide variety of backgrounds congregated. It was in this setting where I matured as a healer and a teacher although I still remained a "spiritual student" who continued to learn from each client I had the honor to serve. Throughout the process, my angelic guides and I were growing together in a mutual partnership of respect and trust. Using my intuitive senses and gathering heavenly and earthly cues, I became capable of making wise, awakened decisions and providing guidance for others.

When I started the day spa and wellness center all those years ago, intuition and mystical spirituality were considered still fringe enough only to be discussed within a closed circle of friends. Currently, there are thousands of books written about angelic beings and their interactions with humans. I consider this to be a wonderful advancement of spiritual inclusion. However, a significant amount of personal effort is required to make use of this knowledge wisely. The messages of angels can have a substantial influence on behavior and actions and it is important to understand one's responsibility when it comes to the human work that is required in manifesting goals. The term "co-creating," which is often seen in modern spiritual literature, refers to the joint endeavor between humans and their spiritual guidance. In order to achieve the desired results and happiness, both human efforts and heavenly resources must be used.

Many are apparently more focused on *hearing* angelic messages rather than carrying out the hard spiritual work that the messages reveal to be necessary. I have to admit that hearing messages is often the fun part of bringing about change and growth. However, when energy from the other side makes itself known, it is for the purpose of illuminating an issue that requires human awareness and attention. More times than not, the guidance calls you to take enormous human risk and to place full trust in yourself, God and the heavens above. It takes time and courage to undertake this inner work.

To envision angelic energies from the other side as co-creators of change in your life requires an open mind and a leap of faith. Ancient religious texts often depict angels as mysterious entities who look upon us from afar. Traditionally, humans pray for their heavenly blessings and wait hopefully for a response while coping with their challenges alone. Fearful of making mistakes, many avoid taking action while waiting for an obvious "sign" from above in order to proceed.

As a teacher, I am always stressing the need to take an active role in your life and your spiritual work. Results are not achieved by sitting back idly and waiting. My personal relationships with the angelic forces from the other side are in some ways like human friendships; although the angels are invisible, they work in tandem with me and are available on a stand-by basis when needed. Some are pretty, tender or motherly types whose role is to console the hurts of human souls. Others are warrior-like, rough in appearance; they push you forward toward greater spiritual rewards. Your guides are available every step of the way to assist in your lessons, yet they never solve or rescue you from your human problems. It's important to remember *not* to rely unquestioningly on the information being transmitted from the other side, and I have never done so. I always evaluate the messages I receive through my intuitive sensing as well as my intellect before acting on any information. For me, this two-way partnership constitutes "co-creating" with the angels.

Co-creating is really a subjective term and it can be applied to many aspects of awakened living. It must be personally defined within the soul of every human heart. One of my favorite books on the subject of angels is Doreen Virtue's *Archangels and Ascending Masters: A Guide to Working and Healing with Divinities and Deities*. This is an insightful guide for anyone interested in connecting with energies from the other side.

My own connections with these energies were strengthened during the years I worked at the day spa. During this time, I also had to learn how to articulate my internal, often ineffable experiences to my clientele. It was a training ground of sorts where I could develop my intuitive talents as well as my communication skills. Eventually, the time came when I was called to share my voice with a larger audience. This came about when a professional acquaintance of mine, who happened to own a radio station, was looking for a part-time host for one of his programs. I would love to say that he hired me for the job because of the wisdom I could impart to his listeners. However, this was not the case at all! He was merely looking for a good on-air talker, and apparently I fit the criteria. A dozen years later I am still hosting my own talk show. This opportunity brought me one step closer to fulfilling the commitment I made to my guides back in college.

Last year I was hosting a radio show series entitled, "Living your Authentic Self." One of the guests on this program was Andrew Harvey, author of *The Hope: A Guide to Sacred Activism*. In his book, Harvey discusses the importance of finding your "networks of grace," a term referring to your spiritual community. At the time I read Harvey's book, I had previously written about my own search to discover a supportive group of like-minded individuals. His wonderful phrase perfectly captured what I had been looking for, and his book put into words the search I had personally experienced.

While my professional life was falling into place at the spa, I still felt a sense of personal sadness or perhaps it was that I felt there was a missing part in my own spiritual story. The feeling would surface periodically but disappear before I did anything about it. This loneliness was my soul crying out to the universe for my own "network of grace." Though I felt the cure for my problem existed somewhere, I was not sure how to find it. In the meantime, I continued to serve my family and my clients at the day spa and prayed for divine intervention.

Eventually, this prayer would be answered. For a number of years now, my family has received the honor of inclusion in a wonderful spiritual community. The blessing grew out of a seemingly "chance" friendship that began during an ordinary day at my workplace. After exiting a treatment room at the spa, I rounded the corner and saw a stunning, princess-like East Indian woman who was waiting patiently for me. Her presence lit up the room, and the entire staff seemed to sense that something special was in the air that day. The workspace was filled with a peaceful vibration, higher than usual, and I sensed that this person had been sent from a higher source.

As soon as we spoke, the two of us hit it off and we connected at once. After several visits together, our professional relationship blossomed into a lasting friendship. During one of her regular appointments at the spa, she thought to present me with a book of East Indian philosophy.

In college I had developed an interest in theology and comparative religion. Still open to this subject matter, I was happy to receive my friend's gift—*Autobiography of a Yogi* by Paramahansa Yogananda. I had previously been exposed to Eastern philosophy through another dear friend of mine, who had been personally mentored by another well-known guru and had gleaned many insights from her travels with him around the world. Eager to learn about Yogananda, I read the book from cover to cover with barely a pause.

Paramahansa Yogananda, an enlightened master from India, had tutored the masses in meditation, the expansion of consciousness, and many teachings that parallel those of Christ. Although he had already passed away long before I read the book, I knew that there were other illumined masters who had been mentored along the same lines of thought.

With thoughts of Yogananda's philosophy filed away in my mind, I carried on with my career, which was now in full swing. I was teaching others how to connect with their intuitive language and to transform their messages into spirit-guided action. My own meditation practice provided me with a sense of deep peace and allowed me to retreat instantly into a zone of pure white light whenever I felt the need. I became able to read and communicate with almost any form of energy from the other side that crossed my path. Though all of this was professionally satisfying, I could not escape the fact that I was still missing a core spiritual essence in my life, my "networks of grace."

Unknown to others, I had a secret, burning desire to rejoin a fellowship of worshipers who would be compatible with my inclusive spiritual ideology. The church had always been my home away from home, and loneliness was easily remedied in those days by sharing a soda pop or two with another church member. But now I was a spiritual servant without a sanctuary. Like hundreds of others, I had stepped away from traditional religious practice in order to independently explore the realm of self-awareness. If the church was not offering spiritual satisfaction to the many who had stepped away, then where were they finding the guidance and incentive to continue their growth? Personally, I felt alone and spiritually homesick. I wanted to find a group where I belonged again.

FINDING MY SOUL FAMILY

Although I felt I no longer belonged in the church of my childhood, I was convinced there was some kind of group that needed me as much as I needed them. My prayers focused on this intention, and I spent many moments listening for an answer.

"Seek and ye shall find." This is what I had been taught at Sunday school, and it still rang true on many levels. After reading the book of Indian philosophy that had been given to me, my relationship with my Indian friend deepened. The book had piqued my interest, and I was eager to learn more about her religious practice. As our trust in each other grew, she began to include me in the small social and spiritual gatherings she hosted. My use of both the words "social" and "spiritual" to describe these events is deliberate, for they truly were examples of "living in the process of God," as discussed in Chapter 8. It was through spending significant time with this group that I began to grasp the concept of artful living. In this community, as in others, the culture encompasses both social and spiritual activities; there is no separation between the two.

As my relationship with my Indian friends grew, I made the decision to bring along my husband and children to one of their gatherings. At first, it felt a bit awkward for all of us. After all, this group of devotees had been together for many years, and my family came from an entirely different faith and religious perspective. However, their gentle acceptance soothed our anxieties. The graciousness they showed me and my family was almost overwhelming, in fact.

Growing up, I had received the message that those who were not devotees to our particular faith could never quite achieve spiritual bliss and would fail to reach the goal of going to heaven. Observing this new group of friends, however, it was apparent that they were filled with joy and gratitude as they lifted their visions to God and gave thankful praise. They did not appear to be missing anything that would suggest they were sad, miserable, or incomplete in their love of spirit. The scenario was forcing me to take a hard, long look at what I thought God's chosen people looked like.

This new group exemplified what it meant to truly dedicate your days to willing servitude toward the glorification of God. They had *it* and the secret of humble service that was completely without ego could be seen in their eyes. I, on the other hand, had only thought that I knew *it*. As one of the "spiritual elite," I had quoted Bible stories and given pat answers to demonstrate to the outside world that I knew the required lessons. This knowledge, however, was intellectual. At this new juncture, I was being asked to truly feel, taste and sense the word of God. The paradigm was right in front of me, and I was now being asked to dedicate my cause to this full expression of faith. It was time to tear down my religious biases and start anew with a fresh worldview of spirituality. As I prepared to take on this task, I realized my prayer had finally been answered: my family and I had found our soul family.

We are a group whose main interest is praising the miracles of life brought forth by the grace of God. Although we are a diverse group of individuals, we are not disgruntled castoffs who separated from our respective religious backgrounds. Nor are we cult-like in our manner of communing together. Individual preferences are respected, and there are no attempts to convert anyone to another faith. We are a group of open individuals who transcend beyond our earthly religious preferences and meet in a realm of spiritual anonymity. We come together to share ancient parables and teachings from all traditions and to meditate in prayer for the greater good of all beings. We strive to model for our children a spiritual worldview of inclusion for all God's people.

For me, personally, the group provides a setting where I am completely embraced and my intuitive gifts are honored as a blessing from above. Finding this "network of grace" brought me spiritually home again to an environment where I could delight in my spirituality. By observing and participating in other spiritual traditions, I learned how to integrate new religious thoughts and ideas without forgetting my own Christian roots.

What has occurred among my soul family has been happening across the globe, as others take part in the "second awakening," in which the glory of God becomes more important than differences of faith. As I consider this movement, I cannot help but think about the origins of the Christian faith. Old ways were challenged as radical new thoughts were put forth and a new doctrine was established. This massive movement occurred as groups of people who sought greater meaning in their humble lives found the courage to break away from the rigid religious dogma of the day. They searched for ways to come together and join with like-minded individuals as they bonded together for a greater religious cause. Gathering in small towns and fields, disciples spoke to awakened listeners who were ready to hear the good news. Initially, they did not have a church or even a structure to shelter them; they had each other and their souls' calls to change the world, one small group at a time.

Searching for Your "Chosen Leader"

All religious and spiritual ideologies encourage their followers to look to their master teacher to guide and support their quest for spiritual wisdom. Among Christians, this teacher would be a minister, priest or leader of the congregation. Similarly, those who seek advice and guidance in the world of business might seek out a "mentor." When searching for a mentor, people normally take time and care if researching the appropriate person to turn to before placing their trust and their future into the hands of another. This same kind of due diligence needs to be applied to one's spiritual life.

Choosing a spiritual master teacher is one of the most important decisions ever made during the course of a lifetime and ought not to be taken lightly. I was amazed to discover how much thought my new group of spiritual friends put into this. For each one of them, choosing a master teacher is a well thought-out process requiring a great deal of soul searching. In order to find the right fit for both student and teacher, they spend a fair amount of reflective time identifying their own spiritual voice and researching a teacher's spiritual lineage. For some, this decision results in a lifetime commitment while others will work with several master teachers throughout the years.

As many people move toward an inclusive worldview of spirituality, the process of choosing the right spiritual leader becomes even more relevant. Stepping away from a traditional religious system allows you the freedom to make spiritual choices of all kinds. However, this freedom can be a double-edged sword. There may be no rules or boundaries holding you back, but this can result in too little or too much exploration. Spiritual growth results from your own incentive to change; the responsibilities that accompany this mind shift can be too much for some to handle on their own. The key is to recognize when you have ventured out too far in either direction of extremes. If you become either too closed in and rigid in your beliefs *or* go too far out and adopt scattered, incohesive ideologies, either can be detrimental to your growth. This is why working with a master teacher who has taken the journey before you is essential. The right person will impart the spiritual and practical wisdom necessary to maintain a healthy balance. Finding this person was a task I undertook, and my spiritual family assisted me in this process.

My spiritual family consists of members from different areas of the world. Being part of this group afforded me the opportunity to sit and meet with enlightened spiritual teachers from a multitude of faiths. Over the years I read about many living illumined masters, but I never imagined I would have the opportunity to meet them. Spending time with an enlightened presence changes you and the way you see the world forever. These individuals have their particular origins of faith, but they have evolved beyond the confines of religion and speak only of love. The subtle evangelical tones to their speech evoke a sense of optimism and confidence. They speak of hope for humankind and the power we all possess to achieve the goals of unconditional love, acceptance, and spiritual neutrality.

After my interactions with these enlightened humans, I was compelled to assess myself and my life honestly. I needed to identify both my strengths and weaknesses and claim all of it as my own. Awakened living is not about accentuating your positive qualities and leaving behind the negatives ones. It is about seeing past our petty traits and idiosyncrasies and discovering the more significant spiritual essence behind our human forms.

It was through this intense soul searching that I began to live from my spiritual center. As the fog began to lift, my meditation became more focused and my vision clear.

Though I continued to listen and interact with the world, I was no longer engaging in the drama of the world. My actions became driven from love and not fear of making mistakes or offending others. After this transition, it was time to find my next teacher. It would be someone who would share higher wisdom, accept my innate spiritual curiosity, and honor my religious lineage.

During meditation, I could sense my teacher's energy coming closer to me. Then there was a moment, a split second, when I saw his face in my mind's eye. I knew it was only a matter of time before we would find each other. Soon enough, a visitor arrived from India. He spoke at a gathering hosted by my spiritual family. The minute I laid eyes on the man, I knew he would play a significant role in my life from that point on.

Since this initial meeting, he and I have spent countless hours in sessions where I was lovingly tutored in the spiritual ways of the world. These are not quiet, solemn meetings, for we are both feisty and headstrong in our beliefs. My mentor's messages carry divine hope for the world and encouragement to claim God's blessings. Both of us believe in the ability of humankind to navigate out of its current trials and tribulations. The way to do to this is through knowing the love of God.

When my master teacher found out that I was writing this book, he granted me the privilege of asking him any questions to help with this process. The question I asked him pertained to finding one's spiritual master teacher. This was his response:

When people choose to become "sannyasins," they must choose their gurus wisely. It is their duty to serve the Lord they come for. They will always give and never take. Enlightenment is not based on religion, though it is proper to have one's own deity. For the true devotee, our language may be different but our quest remains the same. Our bodies may be different but our souls remain the same. We will always have many names to call Lord and only one to call God; that will always be LOVE.

Do not choose your teacher by the number of followers the individual may have. A true guru does not need a thousand disciples. What is needed is an open heart and the willingness to know thyself.

—Swami Mohan Das Bairagi

It has been an honor and a joy to be a student of Swami Mohan. It may seem strange that a Christian minister's daughter has followed this course, but there are no straight paths when it comes to one's destiny and spiritual journey. When you remain open to unlimited choices, the world is full of surprises. My Christian traditions will forever be a part of who I am, and my exploration into the East has only served to deepen my love of God and my desire to be a pluralistic servant of the Lord.

11

Your Spiritual Identity

I am willing to risk exposing my human vulnerability
for the chance to experience the eternal learning
curve of life.

When I began my spiritual journey as a child in my father's church, I was simply following the directives of the adults around me. As an "unconscious servant" I was not always sure why I was asked to perform certain duties, but I was happy in my role. At some point in time, though, it became apparent that I was being called to take a more active role in my spiritual development. I was not alone in hearing the calling from above to keep searching; unbeknownst to me, others around the world were receiving the same intrinsic message and awakening from their unconscious, spiritual sleep.

As they heard the subtle voice of spirit, brave and courageous teachers were stepping forward and planting seeds of spiritual awareness across the land. Leaders such as Neale Donald Walsh, Deepak Chopra, Carolyn Myss and others had discovered ancient spiritual concepts and were presenting them in formats that fit our contemporary times. They shared previously unheard of revelations about the nature of the human spirit. Though many people embraced these messages, others considered it radical fringe thinking to suggest that the mystery of God could actually be found within one's human soul.

Quite a few of the new spiritual teachers suggested that turning your attention from exterior, religious thoughts to interior, intuitive wisdom could lead to a closer relationship with God. They espoused the concept of "heal thyself" and suggested that normal human beings could take an active role in their personal spiritual growth. This movement occurred at a time when many Americans had achieved a level of wealth and physical comfort. Of those who had reached this place of relative security, growing numbers had begun to question the greater meaning of it all. Although worldly success and luxurious possessions had been acquired, there were some who continued to feel a longing within their souls. The new spiritual teachers spoke to these needs and offered the missing piece many had been seeking.

Those who listened to these untraditional and somewhat radical messages started having conversations with others about the possibility of achieving higher states of consciousness and reaping the rewards of spiritual maturity rather than material success. They desired the experience of divine love and joy and questioned the necessity of human suffering. They sought forgiveness for past mistakes and peace with others without having to practice penitence, and they hoped others would obtain the same level of clarity. A concept of universal oneness was also being discovered; the connection between humans, the planet and social responsibility was becoming clearer. The guidance of these key new teachers affected a culture shift that reconfigured the expectations people had for both their religious and spiritual experiences.

These historic changes comprise what I identify as the "first awakening" to spiritual self-awareness. As the exciting new movement progressed, hundreds of people fled their traditional religious communities in pursuit of individual spiritual exploration. They were following the inner calling of their souls to expand their experience of God. Just like intrepid explorers and guides of bygone centuries who forged new paths, they were traveling in uncharted territory. Those who insisted upon strict adherence to religious dogma were not inhabitants of this frontier. In the new land, restrictions were not placed upon religious teachings. Attracted by the promise of spiritual freedom, a considerable number severed ties with their religious institutions and vowed never to return.

I feel fortunate that I have not felt forced to choose between religious tradition and spiritual exploration. To this day, I continue to assimilate new spiritual lessons while remaining connected to my religious roots. However, there were those who felt they were not given this option and they ended up leaving their churches in order to experiment with practices that they hoped would lead to spiritual illumination. Meditation, yoga and Tai Chi became popular and helped fill the void when religious practices were abandoned. A new dimension of spiritual energy permeated the world, and many felt entitled to live their lives and experience God without a sense of guilt. Forgoing the traditional intermediary minister or priest, they thought to travel straight to the source for personal direction and answers.

In conjunction with this spiritual movement, people began seeking new techniques to heal their bodies. Energy work, massage therapy and acupuncture are just a few of the modalities that became more commonplace. Once labeled as alternative medicine by the predominantly allopathic medical community, these options are now considered mainstream in community after community. Helped by nontraditional healing practices, many have felt their energy, their life force, come alive after years of nonuse. As their physical bodies healed, people began to physically sense the energy of the God source within their minds, bodies and souls.

There was no turning back from this glorious, awakened state of grace. The movement was catching on fast as people became determined to take their salvation into their own hands. Established religious organizations were not threatened by these developments. After all, it was still a minority of worshipers who chose to embrace this new way of life. Those who broke with established churches no longer identified themselves as "religious," but rather as "spiritual." A shift was occurring where micro religious thoughts, which focused on the particular tenets of faith, were being replaced by macro spiritual awareness, which focused on the universal experience of divine presence.

SECOND AWAKENING

The spiritual movement has now entered a new phase, one that I consider to be the "second awakening." In this phase, people have come to embrace the natural and healthy exploration of the spiritual self within a relatively brief period of time. This trend suggests that there will be an ongoing progression of awakening. Individuals once excluded for their unconventional beliefs are becoming accepted in an increasingly inclusive world.

What was once considered fringe spiritual ideology has become mainstream thinking. It is now common to see human beings extending their hearts and hands in compassionate acts for others regardless of their religious backgrounds. The possibility exists, more than ever before, of giving and receiving unconditional love. In addition, people are coming to experience a heightened spiritual connection to God that exceeds the limited expectations of the past. The second wave of teachers are building upon the groundwork laid by the spiritual pioneers who went before them and thousands of communities, large and small, are being reached. The evidence for this movement is everywhere: on television, radio and the Internet, as well as in newspapers and magazines. Perhaps most significant are the personal conversations at home.

The days are gone when people lived in segregated religious communities and were able to isolate themselves from outside influences or thoughts. We now live in a global society where there is instant access to information and constant exposure to diverse cultures and spiritual perspectives. Church or spiritual rituals once considered to be private can become instantly known; they can create a ripple effect and influence religious communities clear across the other side of the planet. As we move forward, separatism is no longer a viable option. Myopic views are giving way to greater openness as the world becomes more culturally, economically, and spiritually interconnected. The transformation has reached a critical mass and is now progressing at an accelerated rate. As we are presented with more choices and information, greater personal responsibility is required.

I look forward to the day when the word *tolerance* is replaced by *acceptance* with regard to our discussions of other faith perspectives. *Tolerance* suggests that there is something incomplete or wrong with a group's way of praising God and that the group is graciously being forgiven for its unclean ways. If they are tolerated, they are considered flawed creations. In an ideal world, love would be shown for all, regardless of differences. However, at this point in our spiritual evolution, it is perhaps more realistic to speak of moving from tolerance to acceptance. When we understand that we are all here to learn with one another and from one another, then we move into a state of acceptance of all perspectives and ideologies. After reaching this stage of acceptance, I envision another exciting evolution where the religious and spiritual worlds unite to create a new paradigm of religious spirituality.

Each world religion composes a piece of the mosaic pattern of God.

Each holds an equal value, size, and purpose. There is no reason that one denomination should possess more physical, earthly, or spiritual power over another.

*It is when all the pieces are assembled together that
the perfect reflection of God may be seen.*

Because I have moved into the phase of universal acceptance myself, I often describe my life as that of the *quiet war-
rior*. For many years I strove to maintain a separation between
my professional career and my personal spiritual beliefs but
doing so became a solitary uphill battle. While expressing
nontraditional views can make one vulnerable to criticism, it
has nonetheless been exhilarating to be open in the expression
of my pluralistic, spiritual way of living.

As a pluralistic servant, religious or spiritual biases are
transcended. Intentions for the highest good are held for others as well as oneself. One becomes an active observer as well
as a participant in the human experience, and life becomes an
expression of love and a means of sharing the gifts that have
been given. For me, this involves making use of my intuitive
talents. I have a calling, just as those who are educators, doc-
tors, lawyers or accountants do. How I fulfill this calling is up
to me, just as fulfilling a personal calling is up to all of us. We
are each given our own blank canvases; we are free to paint
an original spiritual work of art and to be whatever we aspire to be. As we move forward in this next phase of spiritual
awakening, it is important to remember that no matter what
happens globally, the work to be done always resides within
the individual.

Never lose sight of the interconnection of all human beings with heaven and earth and more importantly, never lose

sight of their interdependence. It is our responsibility to keep our bodies and minds grounded in the energy of the earth and to keep our spirits aligned with heavenly guidance at all times. Doing so will ensure that we maintain our spiritual innocence, or innate connection to our souls, throughout our lifetimes. Remember to stay connected to Mother Earth, to nature, and to do something as simple as working in a garden or sitting under a tree. The healing energy from the earth will always offer refuge from the chaos in the world.

The soul's desire to know God never ceases, and we must always remain engaged in the process. Whether we like it or not, we must surrender to the fact that life is a series of continuous changes. Lessons will come and go, but the role of the spiritual servant will remain constant. Use your spiritual tools, including your expanding intuitive language, wisely to affect change in the world. Although one's calling needs to be taken seriously, it is important to remember to live with joy, laughter and a sense of abundance.

While your responsibilities in life may feel overwhelming at times, it is helpful to remain present to what is right in front of you. Learning to rise above what is insignificant helps you to identify what is essential and which lessons need to be assimilated. Those who choose to live as pluralistic servants come to realize how their actions and decisions affect the group, how group decisions affect communities, and how community decisions affect the world. We truly live in a world where we are all connected, where we are one.

All of our individual, spirit-guided actions create trails of light and together these represent the higher essence of humanity, or one clear thought of Christ. Having accepted and understood your life's noble mission, let your intuitive sensing remain on "high alert" and let the voice of your soul take the lead at all times.

While feelings of uncertainty might arise during the journey ahead, all who seek to discover their authentic selves and follow the wisdom of their souls will succeed. Those who feel alone and seek to find their spiritual families will also be rewarded. Wise teachers can provide guidance but each individual must never relinquish full decision-making power.

My prayer for the world is that we all come to serve as pluralistic servants of God and to accept the infinite possibilities for our lives and the lives of others. May we embrace each lesson that comes our way, knowing that the soul's voice will lead us to discover our most authentic selves, or who we are within the process of God.

In willing religious servitude we strive to advance along our personal sacred paths.

In willing spiritual servitude we strive to assist others to advance along their sacred paths.

In willing pluralistic servitude we strive to assist the world to advance along its sacred path.

The choice of who we become is ultimately, and forever, ours.

Bibliography

Several of the books listed below were mentioned in *Beyond the Pews*. This brief bibliography is offered to those who wish to read more on the subject of spiritual growth and transformation. From nonfiction to fiction, these titles inspire the mind and nourish the soul.

Chopra, Deepak. *The Book of Secrets: Unlocking the Hidden Dimension of Your Life.* New York: Three Rivers Press, 2005.

Das Bairagi, Swami Mohan. *Self Realization.* Jalandar: Baba Mohan Dass Trust, 1996.

Harvey, Andrew. *The Hope: A Guide to Sacred Activism.* Carlsbad: Hay House, 2009.

Murphy Milano, Susan. *Time's Up: How to Escape Abusive and Stalking Relationships Guide.* Indianapolis: Dog Ear Publishing, 2010.

Myss, Caroline. *Anatomy of the Spirit: The Seven Stages of Power and Healing.* New York: Three Rivers Press, 1997.

Osborne, Mary. *Nonna's Book of Mysteries.* Chicago: Lake Street Press, 2010.

Virtue, Doreen. *Archangels and Ascending Masters: A Guide to Working and Healing with Divinities and Deities.* Carlsbad: Hay House, 2003.

Walsch, Neale Donald. *Conversations with God: An Uncommon Dialogue (Book 1).* New York: Putnam, 1996.

Whitehurst, Ellen. *Make This Your Lucky Day: Fun and Easy Secrets and Shortcuts to Success, Romance, Health, and Harmony.* New York: Ballantine Books, 2007.